Perform As A Leader

Perform As A Leader

The Skills And Strategies
To Take You Where
You Want To Go

Orlaith Carmody

Ballpoint Press

For Gavin, Lorcan, Cormac, Cathal and Aislinn

Published in 2015 by Ballpoint Press
4 Wyndham Park, Bray, Co Wicklow, Republic of Ireland.
Telephone: 00353 86 821 7631
Email: ballpointpress1@gmail.com
Web: www.ballpointpress.ie

ISBN 978-0-99328-92-0-0

While every effort has been made to ensure the accuracy of
all information contained in this book, neither the author
nor the publisher accepts liability for any errors or omissions made.

Book design and production by Joe Coyle,
joecoyledesign@gmail.com

Cover photographs: Orlaith Carmody, by Barry McCall

Printed and bound by GraphyCems

Contents

Acknowledgements

I have found out that you do not write a book on your own. Yes, you do a solo run loading the ideas from your head onto the laptop. But afterwards you need people – good people – who care about you and want to help you get it right. You need them to argue with you, and challenge you, and sometimes tell you things you don't want to hear.

There are so many people who helped me, knowingly or unknowingly, with advice, ideas, experience and recollections. Apologies in advance if you are not mentioned here or in the index. You are hugely appreciated, believe me!

First off to the many leaders who shared their insight and knowledge with me. I learned so much from you as I went along. Then to my publisher, and now friend, PJ Cunningham for his experience and stories. He helped me to craft the idea for the book in the early stages, and kept me on track to get it completed.

Enormous thanks to my readers and 'sense checkers' Brian Coleman and Dearbhla Gallagher – your honesty and direction were terrific – and to the proofing queen herself, Niamh Carmody.

To designer Joe Coyle who is very patient indeed, and to Barry McCall for the photography. To Frances Jones for the styling, and lots of other support that is hard to describe, but very impactful.

Capturing the training and coaching I do in book form has been an ambition for a long time, and it would not have happened without the focus my EO membership gives me, and the personal encouragement from the members of my Forum – Colin Culliton, Pat Doyle, Patrick Joy, Ben McAuley, Paul Molloy, David O'Flynn and Kieran Walsh. I am lucky to know you.

Thanks also to the team at Mediatraining.ie, for taking care of so much detail – Grainne Lynn, Olivia Sunderland, Aldona Fabisiak and John Kavanagh.

Two ladies in my life deserve a very special mention, my mother Blathnaid Carmody and my mother-in-law Ann Duffy, who both come from a long line of great women, and who are an inspiration to all around them. They spend their waking hours giving me encouragement. My wonderful dad Michael is no longer with us, but he taught me to always see the possibilities, and would have loved to have seen this book.

Another special mention goes to my long time friend Helena Mulkerns, who has been nudging me gently towards writing for years.

To my beautiful children, Lorcan, Cormac, Cathal and Aislinn, you are the reason for everything; and to my siblings and extended family on both sides for all the get-togethers and the craic!

Finally, the most important acknowledgement is for my husband and business partner Gavin Duffy. None of it could have happened without you. You are simply the best.

Introduction

How effective are you as a public performer. Do you have the ambition and the know-how to really shine?

In glass buildings all over the world, right now, there are meetings underway, negotiations taking place, ideas being pitched and sales being made. In radio and television stations, spokespersons for business and politics and causes of every kind are talking the talk, trying to sound as knowledgeable and persuasive as they possibly can.

Whether we realise it or not, we are measuring the people doing the talking.

We are appraising them for something intangible and hard to describe, yet something we know instantly the minute we hear it.

We are assessing the performance of leadership.

We are measuring the elusive 'executive presence' so prized in the corporate world; that unique set of markers that allow certain people look, sound and act like leaders, every time they open their mouths.

You know the kind of people I am talking about, and you wonder how they do it:

– You loved his talk and the way he had the audience in the palm of his hand.

– You saw her on a panel debate on television and were impressed with the way she made her points so easily.

– You admire the way he chairs a meeting, getting through the business so efficiently every time.

– She negotiates so well and always comes out with the deal in her hand.

– He inspires and motivates his team to achieve great things.

So here is the critical question.

As a business person, a corporate campaigner, an educator, a politician – in whatever walk of life you currently find yourself – how do you show up as a performing leader?

What is your head telling you right now about how you performed at that meeting last week, or when you stood up and made the presentation, or when you finally got in front of that important client and made the pitch?

Were you as effective as you wanted to be?

Or do you ever think that you are better than you come across? Do you sometimes think your performance is not quite all that it could be?

What? You are saying it is not about performance?

Oh yes it is!

Every time we stand in front of an audience our performance depends on:

- How well we have prepared
- How we are feeling
- How much is hanging in the balance

The outcome from these occasions – for ourselves and the groups and organisations we represent – depends entirely on how we perform in the moment, and how others measure that performance.

So now you are probably wondering is it nature or nurture? Can anyone learn to communicate in an engaging and impressive way, that shouts out competence and credibility every time?

I believe the answer is a resounding yes! That is, if you are prepared to put in the work, acquire some skills, practise well and turn up as a complete professional.

And here is where it starts.

This book is your guide to the critical elements necessary to become a resilient, inspiring and confident performing leader.

Chapter One focuses on self-exploration, questioning leadership and what our understanding of it really is.

Chapter Two deals with self-limiters such as anxiety and nervousness and how we can overcome them and move on.

Chapters Three to Eight cover the main areas for performance development, with a practical step-by-step approach to improving your skills and maximising your potential:

- **Presenting and Public Speaking** – Become the persuasive and engaging speaker you have always wanted to be
- **Contributing on the Media** – Get your message across in an interesting and memorable way.
- **Pitching for Business or Finance** – Learn to really connect with the other side, to win the business or secure the investment
- **Meetings that Make Sense** – Organise, lead and contribute to meetings that are focused, enjoyable, and productive.
- **Successful Negotiating** – Stay calm, take opportunities, and achieve the results you want from every negotiation

- **Become a Coach** – The leader of today is a coach. Learn to spot talent and bring out the best in those around you.

Chapter Nine is aimed at women – and the men who employ them, lead them, follow them, or want to better understand the challenges to full gender diversity.

Chapter Ten is about the decision to lead yourself first, and to find the motivation and the drive to implement the changes that will bring real results.

Over many years of coaching and training in these areas, it has been my absolute privilege and pleasure to help people reach some amazing goals. They have grown great businesses, won large international contracts, achieved significant promotions, delivered TED talks, become brilliant media performers, contributed effectively to parliamentary committees, and delivered inspirational speeches at home and abroad.

With expert guidance and personal focus they learned how to develop and capitalise on their executive presence, and become the performing leaders they always knew they could be.

In *Perform As A Leader* you will find lots of practical advice, and plenty of inside stories from the 'coal face'; from the people who have done it before you. You can put these ideas and strategies to work straight away in your own business or career, to increase your personal effectiveness and to help you achieve your dreams.

Thanks for choosing *Perform As A Leader.* I sincerely hope that you achieve all the success you deserve.

Orlaith Carmody
August, 2015

Chapter One

Leadership

Looking for the leader within.

◆　◆　◆

WHEN I was 25, I was working as a journalist and newly-married to the man of my dreams. Life was about as good as it gets.

But then Kieran, a very fit and athletic 28-year-old – an accomplished rugby and tennis player – began suffering headaches. Various tests were done, inconclusively, and life went on for a while, but one day he suddenly became very ill and was taken to hospital with what seemed to be a fever.

I remember hovering in the corridor as the medical staff came and went, trying to reach his family from an old-fashioned payphone, when the senior duty nurse came bustling towards me.

"You need to contact his family. We are admitting him for more tests," she said. And then after a slight pause, a very curt statement: "You do realise there is a possibility of death here, don't you?"

If lives have a pivotal moment, that was mine; the point where everything you have ever known ends abruptly, and a new normal has to begin.

The corridor tilted into a nightmare of noise and haze as the nurse with the communication skills of a stone yammered right on about the people I should contact, and the things I should do, as I staggered back against the wall, and felt myself slide right down until I was sitting on the floor.

What possessed her, I will never know, to think that bad news should actually be communicated in that way. Or was she so wrapped up in her own busy-ness and routines and self-importance that she never thought at all?

I was picked up off the floor by some junior members of her team who got me a chair and some water, served with big eyes and pale faces, and later I managed to pull myself together so I could tell Kieran's family that he had an inoperable brain tumour.

In the three and a half years that followed, years that we should not have shared if the news I heard that day had been fully accurate, Kieran triumphed again and again and again.

He lost his hair to radiotherapy, his physique to steroids and his mobility to the relentless progression of the illness; but he never once lost his sense of humour or his ability to rationalise and accept each new stage of his life. He never once said 'Why me?' but actually often said 'Why not me?'

He would go a little quiet for a day or two when each new stage arrived, such as using a wheelchair for the first time, but then he would smile his amazing smile and say he had thought about it, he could do it, it was going to be fine.

They were joy filled years during which, despite all that was going on, we managed to travel a little and visit with people a lot; when we had the support of amazing family, friends and colleagues, and when we found in each other the strength we needed to live every minute.

After he was gone, and I tried to make sense of my own life, I took great comfort from the writings of Viktor Frankl, the Holocaust survivor and author of the seminal work, *Man's Search for Meaning*. Frankl's leading premise, on which so much thinking on emotional healing is based, is that we always have the ability to choose our reactions to the things that befall us.

"Everything can be taken from a man but one thing: the last of the human freedoms—to choose one's attitude in any given set of circumstances, to choose one's own way."

So in the depths of the deprivation and horror of the prison camps, he saw people offering comfort and their last piece of bread to another, and he realised that the Nazis could take everything away from them but that choice.

I then understood that Kieran had been doing this all along. He had been choosing to say yes to each new stage of his life and to live it fully, rather than moaning or complaining or becoming angry and resentful.

He was first leading the self, and then leading me to a place where I could accept what had happened to us, and use it to shape my own life ahead. He left me a legacy more precious than diamonds, for which I am more and more grateful every day.

Leadership is the question of the moment, the conundrum of our era.

We are reading about it, and writing about it, and pondering it like never before. And wondering do we have it. Or can we learn it. Or even buy it.

Because it seems to be what you need to get on, these days, in nearly every walk of life.

On a flagship radio programme recently I heard the subject getting a vigorous airing when the host said sceptically, "Oh, come on!" to the business coach he was interviewing when the latter suggested that yes, actually, anyone can become a leader.

But then the host went surprisingly quiet when the coach said he was teaching leadership to new recruits in a supermarket group; school leavers who were going to be stacking shelves and working tills in the immediate future.

But who might learn something about their real potential from the get-go, and develop the ambition to go with the skills learned.

I was impressed with the coach, but even more impressed with the supermarket group, for having the foresight to invest in young people in that way.

We know that there is a leadership shortage the world over. Read any journal from a business faculty, or online article from a research company, and you will learn that baby boomers are retiring in droves. They take away with them heads stuffed full of knowledge and experience, and leave behind a hard-to-fill gap.

The word on the street is that the demand for leadership will far outstrip supply, which is a problem for those organisations losing the years of wisdom along with the grey hair. But it has to be viewed as a major opportunity for anyone ready to grasp the nettle and seriously develop his or her personal leadership skills.

We have all heard the question posed, are leaders born or made? I vote for made, every time.

A whole series of life events have made you the person you are today; experiences which you acknowledge, and apply to the problems and situations you encounter, or which you ignore, packing them into a silo, convincing yourself that they have no bearing on what is happening right now.

I believe it is awareness and ownership of experience that separates those with leadership ability or potential from those without. And this has nothing to do with age or track record, or even status or education.

It has a lot more to do with an understanding of people and situations; intangible skills becoming increasingly more important than tangible in the rapidly changing world we now occupy.

Sure we need the business nous, the technical savvy, the ability to crunch the numbers, to market the products and make the sales. But leadership will really be owned by people who have a deep understanding of how their strengths and weaknesses influence their decisions and behaviours. And how their personal histories impact on everything they do and are.

And before you ask, no, you don't have to lose a partner or a child, or survive a disaster, or climb Mount Everest, in order to find out what you are made of. All you have to do is to dig around a bit, see what is in there, and then make a decision to let it flourish. The leadership seed is right there inside all of us, ready and waiting for a decision to add water, sunlight, oxygen and fertilizer.

So why would you choose to step up to leadership? Why would you bother? We all love honour and glory, and getting a public pat on the back is one good reason.

But often leaders will tell you that these extrinsic factors are not what drive them on at all. They will say their most powerful and authentic motivators are the intrinsic ones – the urge to discover exactly where their leadership gifts are located, and how they can develop them to help others.

They say that their best reward is sharing their knowledge so that others can do well too, and this process often starts inside their own front door.

Warren Rustand, a veteran of over 50 US state boards, and as a young man an aide to President Gerald Ford, believes that leadership starts with the self, goes on to the family, then spreads to the business, and finally to the wider community.

How many people do you come across who are driven, focused 'players' out there in industry, but whose family lives are falling apart, he asks? He believes those people are in denial, lacking in self awareness and authenticity, not acknowledging the trouble their lives are really in.

At a lecture recently in Washington to the Global Leadership Academy of the Entrepreneur's Organisation I heard him say "lead your family" again and again to the assembled entrepreneurs. It was a strong message.

How do you find out what 'authentic' looks like, and how do you access your own authenticity, to put it to the service of others? Because that is essentially what defines good leaders – they are special in their engagement with others, their interest in others, their care for others, and their ability to make others believe in themselves. And, of course, the ability to communicate all that loudly and clearly.

But before we get into the chapters on performance let's have a look at a few personal bases, an understanding of which, and on which, training and development could be platformed.

Authenticity Check

So who are you really? And what do you actually believe? Have there been pivotal moments in your own life that made you realise exactly what matters? Was it a childhood experience, a challenge to your health, a job you got fired from?

What is it that makes you suddenly stop, and take stock of all the things that really matter?

David Hopley, OBE, was a serving Colonel in the British Royal Marines when his youngest son came out as gay in 1998. A motivational speaker and trainer these days, David told me this story about a talk he and his son did together recently.

"I was in denial for many years and it took a special moment to make me realise that I was not living by my values, let alone being the sort of father I should be to a boy I love very much. Anyway, we decided that we would share our journey and the opportunity came to do a session together at a corporate event in the city. With only a loosely agreed outline to guide us, we each introduced the other and ended up speaking for over an hour. There were grown men crying when we finished. It was an amazingly emotionally charged session, and I think the best speech I have ever given."

It is a great example of how you can discover yourself when you are challenged.

In questioning your own authenticity, maybe you have to consider a time when you paid a price for your beliefs, when you went against the tide on grounds of principle. And to ask yourself what was the learning from that episode?

Performing as a leader is putting beliefs and principles into action, owning them and demonstrating them, not stuffing them into a closet. It is being yourself, only more so, and with strategically developed skills.

Finding Motivators

Taking time to consider why you do what you do, asking yourself what are your drivers is a great exercise. Do you go out every day simply to earn a wage, to pay the bills, or do you do what you do for the sake of doing it, deriving satisfaction from the tasks as much as from the result?

The old stick and carrot approach to getting people to perform better has been discredited, and it is now widely held that intrinsic motivators are much more powerful. So companies which have a clear vision, other than profit – or along with profit – are much more likely to attract the best talent, the kind of people who like to come to work every day.

And they know to develop all that good talent by encouraging autonomy, mastery and purpose.

> **Autonomy** – the sense of control over how and when you do tasks
> **Mastery** – the wherewithal to grow your skills for the sense of achievement and delight it can bring
> **Purpose** – the sense of making a contribution, making a difference.

Dan Pink's TED talk on Drive – *The Surprising Truth About What Motivates Us* is well worth a watch, his work the result of many years of research into human motivation, and the obvious mismatch between the human capital practices used commonly in the business world, and the ones that actually work.

My personal favourite motivator is mastery, that feeling you get when you keep working at something, practising it, building up your flying hours, until you know you are doing it really well.

Staying Consistent

Mahatma Gandhi said that: 'Happiness is when what you think, what you say, and what you do are in harmony', or put another way, doing what you say on the tin. Consistency in approach and outlook in a leader is deeply comforting and inspiring to those around them – friends, family, colleagues.

We all find erraticism and mood-swings difficult and deflating, and gravitate towards leaders who are the same wherever they are, in whatever company, and despite whatever challenges they face. We want a leader who clearly has a fully integrated life, and shows up as the same person in each part of it – never accepting that it is OK to be a street angel but a house devil!

Writer and speaker, Declan Coyle, puts this idea really well in his book *The Green Platform*, describing the 'white space' between action and reaction, the moment when you choose your behaviour in any given situation. So you can go off on a rant when things go against you, saying 'they' made me really angry, or you can accept that right in that moment, after the action, you actively chose anger. You could just as easily have chosen a different course.

A while ago I brought my teenagers to hear Declan speak and it was very funny to hear them checking each other afterwards on negative behaviour. GET OFF THE RED PLATFORM, they would remind each other loudly if anyone complained about anything, Declan's wisdom going right into our family lingo.

Staying Grounded

The people close to you keep you grounded, they don't let you lose the run of yourself. They tell you when you are out of order, over the top, losing the plot. But you have to be prepared to listen to them. You have to actively look for feedback, and pay attention to it.

A leader has a loose team against whom he sense checks important things from time to time, and if necessary changes course. No one can do it on their own, not even the most confident among us, and strong and close relationships are a great asset.

These relationships are to be found in spouses, family, colleagues, mentors, walk and talk friends, golf buddies, and so on. They are a vital part of a leader's personal support group.

Working in a television newsroom some years back, I remember seeing a quiet, solid journalist plucked from among the ranks to become an anchor on one of the main news bulletins, achieving overnight fame.

A few weeks later she was swanning around the newsroom, snapping the heads off the sub-editors who prepared the bulletins, aping the worst excesses of a more senior anchor, who was notorious for doing the same thing. Luckily it didn't last long, and she got over herself fairly quickly, and settled back to behaving normally to her colleagues. The older anchor carried right on being colourful, let's call it, until retirement, or so I am told!

Empowering Others

People who are confident in themselves and their abilities instinctively encourage others to emerge. They believe there is room in the world for everyone, even direct competitors, and they are generous with their information, sharing it freely.

They never have to be told to take an interest in those around them, or they never have to fake enthusiasm for someone else's situation. There is nothing worse than a manager with bolted on or manufactured 'concern'. Real leaders care hugely about their colleagues and the work they share.

Their empathy for those they lead is complete, and their self awareness extends to knowing when their own behaviours could be unwittingly preventing others from being their best.

- They never pull the rug from under their people by always having to be the best at everything. They let others shine.
- They don't have to be always 'on' refusing to take time out or holidays. They know that when they are not there, others step up to the mark.
- They don't have the answer to every problem. They let the team work things out for themselves.
- They are not ridiculously optimistic, but instead are realistically positive.

Forbes Magazine recently published an article on the most difficult leadership roles in the world and way up there in the rankings was the presidency of a university, because of the broad range of unmanageable constituencies, all the way from partying students to opinionated department heads.

Brian MacCraith, the President of Dublin City University, laughs when he says that at least 20 well-meaning friends and colleagues sent it on to him to read.

"If I started instructing anybody in this campus in the morning, I'd lose them. You've this role of nudging an amorphous, jelly-like structure along in a direction, and it's all about coaxing, and encouraging, and sharing a vision. It's leadership in that way.

"But it's not like corporate direction. I can't fire anybody. I'm not saying that I want to but you don't have that power. You don't have that control. So you have to move the institution along in a much more nuanced, a much more sophisticated way than you can in a corporate situation.

"You have to be communicating effectively with all tiers of the organisation, but particularly the upper tiers, because you can't do this on your own, and the biggest danger you can have in this role is to get decoupled from your senior teams, from the social networks. Communication is one of the key aspects of the role."

Giving Followership

Some time ago I offered support to someone close to me for a particular project. My offer was heartfelt, deeply meant, and openly offered, but I got a metaphorical door slammed in my face for my trouble, a virtual broken nose. All I gained from the experience was a renewed understanding of the following:

You can't achieve a single thing in business or in life without leaders, but leaders can't achieve a single thing, or even exist, without followers.

My friend, by the way, is still struggling away on his project alone, leading neither himself nor anyone else!

The difference between average leaders and great leaders is that great leaders understand followership. They know the road, because they probably gave a lot of exceptional followership on their way to leadership.

To be an effective follower, according to the scholar Robert Kelley and expert on the subject, you have to be enthusiastic, ambitious, intelligent, and self-reliant which sounds a bit like a leader, really.

One of the things Kelley lists as critical to followership is courage – a clear moral compass and the ability to uphold ethical standards, even when superiors are looking like they might be about to do something dodgy.

Ask yourself this. Can you speak truth to power? Or do you

become strangely compliant the closer you are to the centre of control? In other words, can you knock on the door of power, and tell them the house is on fire?

Sinead McSweeney is currently the Director of Public Policy for the EMEA region for Twitter. In her previous roles as Director of Communications for the Police Service Northern Ireland, and separately for the Gardai, and before that a ministerial advisor, she saw plenty of occasions when speaking up was vital.

"The greatest value an adviser can offer is to be authentic and honest in their advice and feedback. Leaders who attract or deliberately surround themselves with advisers who merely mirror or echo their opinions do themselves a disservice and are poorer leaders for it.

"An adviser should be willing to challenge the status quo, critique ideas, and provide constructive advice and feedback. Those who settle into the comfort of being 'agreeable' are diminishing the value of their role," she says.

Good followers also have commitment to the common goals of the team or project, their enthusiasm obviously motivating others. They manage themselves well, so tasks are safe in their hands; and they are hungry for self-development, always seeking out the next piece of the jigsaw, the skill that can be honed or developed.

Producing Results

People who get things done stand out. Task completion ability is one of the things teachers look out for as a marker of those children who are 'most likely to succeed'.

After education, it is still a marker – the people who see the opportunity, get the ducks in a row, get people and finance on board, and produce a result are the ones we read about, write about and like to follow.

Productivity training and coaching is a great way of upping your game in this area, particularly on the technology side, where heaving inboxes and electronic messaging makes it very hard to escape the devices, and the feeling that you have to be 'always on'.

Productivity coach Ciara Conlon, author of *Chaos To Control*, puts email taming at the heart of all her work.

"We live in the age of distraction where constant connectivity both enables and disturbs us from the work we need to do. If you can take control of your digital world by de-cluttering and organising your apps, your email and your social media accounts for easy access and minimal overload, you will experience a calm control that will actually seep into other areas of your life".

Her systems really work, and have certainly made me more productive.

Giving Back

While chairing a strategy day in Galway last year for an engineering firm we were discussing social responsibility and giving back when a participant asked me, how are we possibly supposed to find time for that along with running the business, the family, the home and all the rest of it?

And we agreed that the day you are at your most snowed under, your most overwhelmed, your farthest behind, is the very time you should make that call, or put something in motion for someone else. Because the lift you will get from doing it will make your own stuff suddenly seem so much easier to tackle.

Legendary US radio host Bernard Meltzer said: "There is no better exercise for your heart than reaching down and helping to lift someone up."

And the science seems to back him up with studies showing that volunteering boosts your immune system, makes you fitter and stronger, and allows you to live longer. The theory is that being 'others' centred, channels well-being back to yourself; the 'helper's high' giving you extra energy and optimum performance.

It is also found to reduce depression and anxiety; the sense of usefulness and achievement clearing away obstacles and allowing you forge ahead with renewed purpose.

Studies show that teens and young adults who engage with the concept of give-back become happier and more optimistic, with better exam results and lower substance abuse or anti-social behaviour.

So there is a lot to be said for it.

Interestingly, you will see companies that are beginning to understand the benefits of becoming purpose maximisers as well as profit maximisers, subtly shift their mission statements to imply that profit is the happy result of purpose, and not the only goal.

Leading Your Family

As the 'rags to riches' entrepreneur Jim Rohn once said, you are the average of the five people you spend most time with. So your family – biological or those you have chosen to share your home and your life with – are big influencers on you, and you on them. The journey you share aligns you in thought and purpose, whether you are conscious of that or not.

Handily enough in my own case we are a family of six, so it is very easy for me to name my famous five – my husband and business partner, Gavin Duffy, and our four young adults Lorcan, Cormac, Cathal and Aislinn.

A while back someone introduced us to the idea of Family Forum, where you meet as a family and discuss what's on your mind at regular intervals. We are finding that it is teaching us, the parents, that we must actively work on all the bases mentioned above if we want to allow our kids to blossom.

We have to shut up and listen, and to try to stop giving them instructions all the time. We have to stop being judgemental, stop correcting them and stop criticising them.

We have to start trusting and respecting them, listening to their views and opinions with open minds, giving them the space to tell us what is going on in their lives, without immediately rushing in to fix it or change it. And most importantly, guaranteeing them confidentiality. What comes into the room stays in the room.

Adults often wonder why young people don't communicate? Well, wonder no more. We are the problem. We actively stop them from doing so.

Every parent wants their kids to have more than they did, to be better educated, to be taller, to have straighter teeth, to achieve more. So we bombard them with instructions on how we think they should get there, instead of letting them work it out for themselves, with the support of a family and a forum that listens.

◆　　◆　　◆

The first time we introduced 'Forum' at home, we got a few strange looks. They want us to do what? Have a meeting? With an agenda and everything?

There were a few comments along the lines of, 'Mam, Dad – this is a family you are running, not a business.' But actually, building a great family is the same as building a great business, it doesn't happen by accident.

Forum very quickly became a part of what we do, an occasion to look forward to, an opportunity to count on. Mind you, I am not sure what will happen when partners come along. We'll have to make that one up as we go along!

Chapter Two

The Performance Audit

In this chapter we have a look at our personal communication, and delve into the things that make us look and sound like a leader. We also consider what prevents us from taking the opportunity to step up and shine, and we analyse and deal with nervousness.

♦   ♦   ♦

I REMEMBER thinking when the memoir of the late and much admired journalist Nuala O Faolain was published some years back, that the title she had chosen, *Are You Somebody?* was a little bit of magic. With searing honesty, she shared enormous doubts about her own contribution to the world, despite having been a very successful columnist and radio producer.

Her book was a runaway bestseller, touching a chord with people all over the world who felt as she did and, I am sure, hugely appreciated the honesty of a public figure baring all.

Nuala's doubts are shared by most of us if we are honest enough to admit it. No matter how well we craft our front, our outward face, there are times when we feel alone and struggling and we wonder if we are making any kind of difference at all.

I love that tee-shirt you often see people wearing in ski resorts, the one that says: 'If you ain't scared, you ain't ski-ing'.

Pottering around the blue runs for an hour or two and then heading in for a hot chocolate is all very pleasant, but it is never going to up your game. Unless you push yourself, and take on the red and then the black slopes, and some day the off-piste, you will never learn, or grow in skill.

It might require scaring yourself a bit, making your heart race, but the exhilaration afterwards and the sense of achievement is just incredible.

Performing as a leader is all about pushing your limits; putting your hand up, stepping up to the plate, and taking action – the very action that might lead to failure, or might lead to great success.

Working with a group of senior female managers in a bank recently, we were discussing performance at the front-line, and I was challenging them to honestly assess their personal performance on different bases.

One manager said that she sometimes had trouble stating clearly where she stood on a particular issue. She said she was inclined to wait and see how others were thinking before revealing her position. She was concerned that this was making her appear weak, or uncertain.

The other managers then chimed in that they too had stayed quiet, on occasion, when they should have owned their positions confidently and clearly.

We did some exercises around firstly working out what your position actually is, and secondly how to contribute in a way that will be impactful, and will persuade others to your way of thinking, techniques that are covered in the chapter on meetings.

Meetings, presentations, negotiations and pitches are the front line – the place where you have to put up or push off. Two more bases of extreme importance are the way you show up as a coach, and how you play out on the media. To my mind, these six skills are vital, and the good news is that they are infinitely learnable and applicable – once you get over the know-do gap.

In *The Knowing-Doing Gap*, Jeffrey Pfeffer and Robert I. Sutton provide a great description of the organisational paralysis that sees eye-wateringly large sums spent on consultants, and then not a single recommendation implemented.

They talk about the months and years of person hours spent on strategy summits and organisational realignments, complete with slide decks and fancy bound planning documents – the perpetrators thinking that all the talking and report writing constitutes real action.

We did a report and there were lots of findings. How often have you heard that?

But those people are actually crippled by fear. Any action risks failure, so the best thing to do is to put the report on the shelf and not actually do anything. If you do, you risk censure, the criticism of colleagues, loss of face, loss of position.

The opportunity to develop and communicate best practice across an organisation is completely lost in a cloud of fear, and a cloud of individual reluctance to stand up and be counted.

But the fact that you are reading this suggests that you want to be different, that you want to check in on your skill sets in these areas to see if you have kept up to speed. Learning is layered, as you well know, and we all have to keep adding to it to keep it fresh.

And if you are at an early stage in your career, it is terrific that you are thinking about these things already. Practice certainly does make perfect, and getting performance miles on your clock is what it is all about.

In doing a personal performance audit across the bases mentioned we have to consider how we show up; how alive, present, engaged, mindful, in the moment we are on a day-to-day basis.

How prepared are we? How do we deliver? How do others rate us? How do we translate all our management learning and university study into practical performance at the front line?

If you find that your performance is less than you would want, is it your fault or that of your organisation? Definitely, there are organisations which seem to suck the life out of individuals; which lack the ability to take the collective knowledge of its people and turn it into positive action.

But there are also lots of organisations who manage to get great results out of very ordinary people, usually by having a strong learning culture, and by using the oldest training method in the book – hear one, see one, do one. So you read about or study a great presentation or pitch, then you go and watch one, and then you do one yourself.

Ultimately we are all fully responsible for our own communication. If I give a pitch to a client, and it falls flat, I can't go back to the office complaining that 'they didn't get us' or 'they didn't understand the concepts'. If they didn't understand every word I was saying, it is 100 per cent my fault. The responsibility to make them understand lies with me, not with them.

The Dreaded Nerves

So what is holding you back from front line performance? From putting yourself forward to do the media interview, or take on the keynote speech? Is it perhaps anxiety? A concern about how you will look and sound in front of colleagues, how you will acquit yourself, how you will deal with the pressure of the moment and the rows of faces looking up at you expectantly?

Everybody gets nervous before a major event, even the most experienced of public performers. If they tell you they are not nervous, they are lying! They are definitely feeling the impact of the adrenaline rush, but what they have learned to do is to channel it in the right direction, and to use it as fuel.

Mastering nerves is the art of first understanding the symptoms, then minimising them, and then developing a system to turn them into performance energy.

Ronan O'Gara, fly-half for both Ireland and Munster for many years, and the fourth most capped player in rugby union history, had the most outstanding focus every time he took a penalty kick. You could see the intense concentration on his face as he placed the ball, went through a set pattern of steps, and took his shot with unbelievable accuracy. You knew that a bomb could go off in the stadium at the same time, and he wouldn't hear it.

He was in a state of Flow, as described by Mihaly Csikszentmihalyi: "A sense that one's skills are adequate to cope with the challenges at hand, in a goal-directed, rule-bound action system that provides clear clues as to how well one is performing".

Flow is that state of intense happiness that comes about when you are on a roll, you have done the prep, you are up to the task, it all goes to plan, and you are delivering the performance of your life. It is a high, almost a euphoric state, an optimal experience.

It comes about as a result of using systems, building skills, focusing intently, cutting out distractions, and quantifying results.

The systems are what this book is about, straightforward steps towards building the skills that will allow you to perform to a higher level than ever before. And it will show you how and where to focus, so the distractions are eliminated.

Hopefully, you will start to get the results you need, and will be encouraged by those results to stay on this great journey of achieving excellence in leadership performance.

So let's start by looking at the physical symptoms of nervousness, the things that hit you in that moment when you go up on stage, or stand up in the boardroom to make the most important pitch of your career. Most people say they experience a selection of the following in the moments before they are due to start:

- Shaking hands
- Tapping Feet
- Dry mouth
- Butterflies in the tummy
- Faster heart beat
- Perspiration
- Distorted hearing
- Distorted vision

They are all caused by the same thing – the fight or flight drug, adrenaline. It is an evolutionary adaptation to allow the body to react quickly to danger; the hypothalamus instantly signalling the adrenal glands to release adrenaline into the blood stream, causing blood vessels to contract in the extremities, redirecting the blood to the heart and lungs to increase physical performance.

Have you ever been checking your mobile device in the car – illegally – and nearly run up the back of the car in front? The hairs on the back of your neck stand up as the adrenaline floods your body in a nanosecond. It is unbelievably fast and equally powerful.

Athletes often call it the 119 per cent drug because strength and speed increase, while the body's ability to feel pain decreases, allowing those phenomenal performances to be pulled out of the bag on the day of a big event.

The problem with boardroom or public speaking performance is that our bodies are preparing for physical danger, sometimes from the day before! They don't realise that we are not being threatened by wild animals or a marauding army. The threat is psychological, and not physical – the psychological threat of failure, shame, reputational damage, or criticism.

In the boardroom, we don't actually need our hearts pumping twice as fast as normal, and our lungs gobbling up air like it was going out of fashion.

But if we learn to welcome the adrenaline rush as an asset, an ally there to help us, it becomes easier to control.

So, on the morning of the big event, you wake up with that feeling in your stomach, and the racing effect beginning. Before you even get out of the bed do these things:

- Remind yourself that this is the cavalry riding over the hill to help you. Tell yourself this is good. Really good. If you listen hard enough, you will even hear the bugles!
- Now remind yourself of the preparation you have done for the event. You have the best possible material gathered, a great structure worked out, and you know exactly where you are going with the message.
- Now focus on the task ahead – delivering the message to the audience in a way that they will really understand and buy into. Remember actor Ed Harris playing Eugene Kranz in the movie *Apollo 13* – "I believe this will be our finest hour."
- Imagine the end result, your objectives achieved. Hold the thought, and get on with your day.

Do you remember 'Bottler,' the scruffy schoolboy character brought to the stage and screen by the comedian Brendan Grace? In his short trousers, twisting his little cap in his hand, 'Bottler' always started his monologue by saying bashfully, 'Yous' is all lookin' at me'.

And that is nervousness right there, that moment when we suddenly realise that everyone will be looking at us.

It is the moment when we focus on our ability to do the task, and forget to focus on the task itself.

You will be hard put to find a better definition of nervousness. The trick with all performance is to mentally turn the spotlight in the other direction, and to make the communication all about the audience and their needs, not about yourself.

On the other hand if we allow the emotional response of the adrenaline rush to be one of panic, and we don't mentally manage it and acknowledge it, guess what happens? Our bodies decide that we didn't get enough adrenaline the first time, and very helpfully send us another shot, the second dose strong enough to fell an elephant!

This can result in light-headedness, dizziness and actual changes in vision, the effect lasting for up to an hour.

And you were thinking of performing with all of that going on?

So the key to the emotional management of adrenaline, before we get to the physical management, is to welcome it and to remind yourself to stay task and result focused – not to get bogged down in negative thoughts like:

'Am I good enough for this task?'

'Should someone else on the team be doing it?'

'I'm bound to screw up.'

'Will they like me?'

'My accent is hard to understand.'

'I wish I didn't use so many ums and ahs.'

'The sales manager is out to get me.'

'I wish I didn't have a spot on my chin.'

All of these thoughts turn the giant imaginary spotlight inward, and can destroy a performance by altering the whole focus of the presentation or communication. The physical symptoms of the adrenaline rush are very manageable too – once we know why they are happening, and once we learn to use adrenaline as it is supposed to be used, to help us and not to hinder us.

Shaking Hands: The rush of blood to the vital organs, to help with slaying potential dragons, leaves our extremities deprived. Have you ever cringed as a nervous colleague stumbles with the mouse, and goes five slides forward, then three back, stuttering and apologising and getting redder and redder in the face?

The poor thing doesn't realise that his fingers are slightly numb. He knows how to use a mouse – he uses one every day – he just can't feel it properly this day, because of the pressure of the occasion.

Before you start a big presentation, you have to physically tell your brain that your hands are still working – 'It's fine, I understand this stuff, I definitely do not need more adrenaline, thank you.' Before every important speech, Bill Clinton used to dig the thumbnail of one hand into the palm of the other, and then reverse it, to tell his brain that his hands were fine, and to instantly remove any suggestion of a shake.

On a stage, the last thing you want to see is shaking hands, or the opposite, a white knuckled death grip on either side of the podium.

Tapping Feet: At the start of a race, before the runners get down to the blocks, what are they doing? The are jumping around, slapping their sides, doing kicks and hops and mini sprints – physically telling the brain that the extremities are in good working order. They haven't gone away.

In the same way, experienced speakers will be pacing in the green room before the conference, walking up and down to focus their thoughts and manage their brain/feet messaging.

At the podium, feet that haven't first been reconnected with the brain, will respond to regular check-in signals by making you tick-tock from side to side, or lean forward and backward, both of which make you look shifty, and far less credible.

Some of the most comfortable speakers in the world abandon the podium altogether, and use movement to help hold on to the audience. But more about that later.

Dry Mouth: Is your mouth really dry, or does it just feel like that? Remember the hairs on the back of the neck in the driving incident? Your neck and throat area are highly sensitised in an adrenaline rush, because they are very important areas to protect during fight or flight.

You are really aware of them now, in a way that you are not usually. So the normal, regular re-salivation you do during conversation hundreds of times a day now becomes 'clicky' and noticeable.

The trick is to hydrate well before the speech or presentation, and it will be less of a problem. Sip water in the green room for a while before the event, not coffee or cola.

Butterflies in the Tummy: You know the feeling, the stomach fluttering and churning causing an unpleasant discomfort and for many, a scramble around the desk drawers for the antacids.

What has happened is that the digestive tract has had some of its normal blood supply diverted to the heart, and the digestive acids are left to have a field day, gnawing away at the lining of your stomach. The coffees and the colas before the event make this much worse.

I find it very hard to eat properly before a big event, so I go for something light and protein based – scrambled eggs or yoghurt are good for me – but it is important to find something that works for you and settles you down.

Faster Heartbeat: The blood that has left your stomach has gone straight to your heart and, as the entire body is over sensitised, you can hear it loudly and clearly. Imagine if you could hear your heart like that all the time. You would never get any work done, or get any sleep.

No one else can hear it, but the racket it is making is seriously distracting, and is making it so hard to do as I have suggested above, to focus on the audience and the message and not the self.

Every part of this adrenaline rush is screaming at you to focus on the self. But maybe now that you know what is happening, and why it is happening, it might be a bit easier to control.

Perspiration: So you are in the middle of the talk, and you suddenly realise you have a bead of perspiration running down your side, tracking its way from rib to rib, under your shirt, to land who knows where. The big spotlight has just been taken away from the audience again, and turned back on to the self.

But here is the thing. No one else actually knows about that rogue bead of sweat. In fact, it is probably there every day of the week, particularly during the summer months, unnoticed, getting on with its job of cooling you down.

In your adrenaline induced heightened sensitivity moment, you feel it, you notice it, and you start confusing your brain by thinking about it. Forget it, get on with the talk.

Distorted Hearing: This is the 'bomb going off in the stadium and the player hearing nothing' moment. That dulling of external, unnecessary noise, and the ability to focus on the moment, is the source of 'Flow'.

Used correctly it is a huge asset. Misunderstood, or used incorrectly, it is a source of sheer panic and yes, you guessed it, a signal to the body to land in more adrenaline, the second dose the one that makes think you are actually going to collapse.

Distorted Vision: It is sometimes called 'threat locking', that sensation where the rows of faces blur in front of you, but you can see as clear as day the person in row 13 who you think dislikes you, or who is your main competitor.

Internalised, this moment becomes all about you and your ability to perform. Externalised, this sharp focus is what makes

Ronan O'Gara hit his target, and what can make you really see and feel what it is your audience wants and needs, right at this moment, to make this whole experience for them, and for you, get into 'flow'.

How To Fix Nervousness

There are many other symptoms of nervousness and adrenaline-rush aside from the ones described here, and they each have a very good physiological reason for occurring. The good news is that once they are understood, they can be dealt with, and the energy generated used as a force for achievement.

So we 'fix' nervousness firstly by preparing in advance for our known and usual physical manifestations of it, and secondly by giving our brain tasks during the performance to keep it externally focused.

Unfortunately, during many of our key performances – pitching for a really important piece of business, making a significant speech, presenting to a room full of colleagues and peers – we do not trust our brains, so we give them far too little to do, and they begin to work against us.

Here is what happens.

Earlier I described the 119 per cent state in which you are operating at this crucial time, assisted by the wonder drug, adrenaline. Your brain is as sharp, focused, and geared up for action as it has ever been in its entire life. And what do you do? You decide to use the great big idiot board known as power point, where the only thing your brain has to do is to read from slides, using up maybe 20 per cent of capacity.

What happens to all the spare capacity? Your brain now becomes your worst critic, starting a running commentary on how badly you are presenting, how poorly the audience is reacting, how badly prepared your slides are, and horror of horrors, is that a typo I have just spotted?

How often have you heard a presenter say:

- 'I'm not sure if you can see this graph' (Of course I can't at the back of the hall!)
- 'I'll just skip a few slides' (So why are they there in the first place?)
- 'You may not be interested in this' (You think?)
- 'You'll see from the bullet points here.' (No I can't, I don't have bionic sight!)
- 'And the bullet points here' (You mean there's more of them?)
- 'There is probably too much detail' (So why the hell is it there!!)
- 'I'm not sure what I was going to say about this slide' (I've lost myself now)

This, tragically, is a presenter becoming deeply self-conscious about his own presentation, and worse still, chronically unhappy with it – his own brain beginning to campaign against him, because he just did not give it enough to do.

And at this point, when he realises that he has locked himself into a relentlessly rigid format, where slide 13 has to come after slide 12, and slide 28, sadly and tragically, has to come after slide 27, he begins to crumble in front of our eyes. He has no way out, and no means of getting back to what the audience wants or needs.

This is truly Death by Powerpoint.

The alternative is to trust your brilliant, fantastic and enormous brain to do the job it was designed to do, particularly when your system is full of adrenaline. You set it tasks to focus on, tasks that are all about delivering a presentation that is audience rather than self led, and you achieve them by working from the correct part of your memory.

Learned Versus Personal Memory

The linear presentation described above will be flat, dull and boring for a lot of reasons, not least because the presenter can't possibly show or produce the best part of himself in that format. Even those who are completely comfortable with slide presentations, and who don't get fussed up or bothered by nerves, will completely close off their communication.

The reason is that learned memory is like a drawer in a filing cabinet, with the information stored in a certain order. And we can only access the information in the same order in which we stored it in the first place.

So if you remember when you were at school, and you were asked by the teacher to recite, you stood up at your desk and began your poem, this one by Robert Herrick:

> *'Fair Daffodils we weep to see*
> *You haste away so soon*
> *As yet the early-rising sun...'*

And then you got the brain freeze and said: 'Sorry Teacher, I'll have to start again', and this time you take a really good run at it and get a bit further.

> *'Fair Daffodils we weep to see*
> *You haste away so soon*
> *As yet the early-rising sun*
> *Has not attain'd his noon.*
> *Stay, stay until the hasting day*
> *Has run to the even-song*
> *And having pray'd together,*
> *We will go with you along.'*

It only works if you take it all together at a run. Don't ask me to pick a word in the middle, and try to start reciting from there. My brain can only access the verse in sequential order.

The other interesting thing about learned memory is how I can't possibly make eye contact with you while I am accessing it. As I pause and go looking for the words, my eyes will go off up to the sky, as if it is from there I have to pull the information down.

When I get the information, I can only deliver it in a sing-song, obviously recited tone of voice, and if I lose my place, I am completely goosed, and may well freeze and completely embarrass myself.

So the sequential format of a slide deck, even where we are really accomplished presenters, locks us into learned memory, information that we can only deliver in a rote way, which makes us stilted and formal, and reduces the chance of any fluency, fluidity or any interactivity with the audience.

Add to that the 'theatre effect' of a formal presentation – the audience sitting back and expecting a show, becoming passive and non responsive – and you are really making your work difficult for yourself.

In fact using learned memory takes up so much of our concentration, that we sometimes shut out that pesky audience altogether, and focus completely on reciting facts and figures, without any reference to relevance, or to the capacity of the audience to take any of it in.

Using predominantly learned memory formalises our language, and our whole demeanour, body language and appearance, and drops us down to the very bottom rung of the communications ladder. This is the one that loudly tells the audience that now is a great time to zone out and start thinking about what they will have for dinner.

Certainly, reciting a few lines of a verse is a device that can be used very well in a presentation, as long it is clearly flagged as a pause for thought.

But a whole presentation that relies on learned memory is doomed to failure. It will fail because it puts the presenter in the wrong place, it puts the audience in the wrong place, and it puts the messaging in the wrong place.

Personal memory, on the other hand, makes our communication come alive; it's the part of our brain and memory usage that shows our personality and it clearly gives the audience the 'why' they should listen to our message, long before we expect them to follow the nuts and bolts of the 'how'.

Personal memory is all about our personality, knowledge, insights, and understanding; the things the audience actually came out to hear.

We never lose our place or get stuck in personal memory and we never lock out the audience. We use conversational every-day language when we are in personal memory, we use colour and description, we tell stories and hold the attention, and we bring our communication right up to the highest rung of the ladder.

Personal memory is that moment when someone who has been giving a fairly dry talk, or reading tonelessly from something prepared, suddenly puts down the script and says: 'You know, what I really want to say to you today is....'

And just watch the room go silent, and the eyes come up from the phones.

We all know something good is coming and we pay attention.

The great Irish actor Eamon Kelly understood that the role of the story teller or Seanchaí was to keep people enthralled, and to bring people real news – in those days long before the internet or even TV or radio. All his stories came straight from personal memory, keeping them lively and in the moment.

In one scenario, the Seanchaí is drawing a map of New York on the hearth of the cottage in which he is sitting, using the ashes from the fire and a poker. An early version of the flip chart, you could say.

And as he explains where cousin John is living now, and where Betty's son Paul is headed, to a rapt audience, a cat leaps into the middle of the picture, scattering the Bronx and Staten Island all the way to New Jersey.

The simple story and dramatic effect has relevance, urgency, unpredictability.

The art of good communication is giving a series of those moments, and having the confidence to reveal the authentic self while doing do.

In performance audit terms, these are the questions we have to ask ourselves about how we have been showing up in the past, and how we are going to do it differently in the future.

- Are we really reaching the audience every time we speak?
- Are the meetings we attend productive and effective?
- When it is our turn to chair, are we doing it effectively and efficiently?
- Are we leading and coaching our teams to success?
- Are we pitching the business in a way that is really connecting with the customer or the potential investor?
- Are we comfortable taking media opportunities?

In the next few chapters, I will show you exactly how you can up your game in all of these areas so you can always perform as a leader.

Chapter Three

Presenting And Public Speaking

In this chapter you will find everything you need to prepare and deliver a great talk. You'll understand the speaker/audience dynamic, the things that go wrong, and then you'll have a blueprint to follow to make sure your own next outing is nothing short of stellar!

◆   ◆   ◆

HE is a tech multi-millionaire who travels the world keeping up with all his investments, and who gets asked to deliver keynote speeches quite regularly.

He came bounding into our offices in Dublin one day looking for help with a presentation he was making in China the following week. He was due to have a 20 minute slot, in front of an international audience.

"I have 68 slides in my deck," he told me cheerfully.

Oh, help us all, I thought, it is going to be a long morning.

So over the course of that session and another one a couple of days later, we completely re-worked his presentation. He ended up with something good, aimed specifically at his audience, and with some very clear easy messages for them to take away.

Oh yes, and I allowed him to keep eight slides! It was plenty.

Ever since we first sat around a campfire and began telling stories, we have honoured and respected those who can capture the human condition and share it with the rest of us.

We fall silent and listen to those who can move or inspire or inform or delight us with their choice of words and their command of language. We can become absolutely mesmerised when the orator also understands and uses body language, facial expressions, gestures, stage-craft, audience skills, pauses, vocal inflections, humour, drama – and a whole raft of other effective tools there for the taking.

The problem is that a lot of people don't bother with these tools, and rely instead on hiding behind the dreaded slides, as we discussed in the last chapter, sending us all to sleep before the third bullet point is on the screen.

My other personal pet hate is the presenter who starts his talk by telling us what he is going to tell us, how he is going to tell it, and what reaction he expects us to have. This is a dreary kind of housekeeping that announces loudly to us that right now is a very good time to do some texting or check emails.

It was a format for starting a talk that was suggested by Dale Carnegie back in the 1950s and it is quite extraordinary that some presentation trainers are still telling people that it works today. Believe me, it doesn't.

Remember Renée Zellweger's great line from the movie *Jerry Maguire* where she played opposite Tom Cruise: "You had me at hello"?

That's how you need to start a talk or presentation for those of us who live in the 140 character, give-it-to-me-up-front world of today. You need to grab our attention from the get go, make us believe in you, and then take us on a compelling journey.

Presenting and speaking is a learned craft. No one did it brilliantly the very first time they stood up there and tried. But absolutely everyone can raise their bar and improve substantially. It takes a few techniques, some practice and a good understanding of how to control nerves, as described already.

A 'feel the fear and do it anyway' kind of attitude helps too.

I was coaching a woman one time who was the second-in-command in the marketing department of a multinational. She decided that for her own career progression she ought to step up and make the main presentation at the annual conference, a role that her team lead had undertaken in the past few years.

So she went up to the CEO to put the case, a little nervously, that her colleague had done the job very well last year, and the year before, and that it might be time to have a fresh presenter with fresh views?

Without batting an eyelid the CEO said yes, absolutely, great idea, the job is yours this year, and don't worry, I'll square it with the team lead.

My friend left the office, and actually had to lean up against the wall outside because of the wave of panic that almost knocked her over. She had not expected to get a yes to her proposal so easily, and having never spoken in public before, now had to deliver in front of a tough audience of her peers.

So we worked hard on the presentation, and got her a practice run in front of a small but very supportive business network. And then she did the presentation at the conference, in front of 300 people, to a great reaction.

She was absolutely thrilled that her decision to push herself, and to put in the work, achieved her goal of raising her personal profile within her organisation.

The Key to a Good Speech

All good presentations and speeches begin with one essential piece of understanding, and that is the fact that we absorb, understand and remember spoken communication very differently to how we absorb written communication.

So think about this for a moment. If you carefully research and write up a paper, intended for publication, and read it out verbatim at a conference, don't be surprised to look up from your reading to find your audience nodding off to sleep, checking mobiles or even getting up and leaving half way through.

You are asking them to do something they are not physically equipped to do – to absorb aurally material that you carefully designed to be absorbed visually and analytically.

The exceptions in your audience are those who have pre-read your paper and have made notes, so they can ask intelligent questions or indeed challenge the content of your paper. They might be relied on to give you a bit of eye contact. As may the few who have the paper printed out in front of them and are reading along with you.

So if this is the case, how then do audio books work? Or how do the visually impaired learn from the written word?

Well authors of popular novels, the kind that are often found in audio book form, are usually great story-tellers. Their narrative style and choice of words is deliberately lyrical, descriptive and colourful, giving us a very full sensory experience. We do not only understand the words, we are prompted to paint pictures in our own heads, bringing the characters, places and scenarios to life.

Add to that a good recording from a skilled actor as narrator, and you layer on the potential for plenty more interpretation and meaning.

And compare that now with my hapless academic and his paper, wondering why the tops of people's heads are the only thing he can see in the auditorium.

He is working with material that is probably very worthy, but on the dry side, and he does not have the descriptive skill of the novelist, or the delivery skills of an actor. So he doesn't stand a chance.

To turn a paper into a decent talk he needs to do the brave thing and leave the script back home on the desk. He needs to work from personal memory and create for the audience an aural experience that will pull them in with pictures and emotion and connection, so they will look up and start listening.

The same goes for the corporate presenter who thinks it is all about the slide deck. She is also asking her audience the impossible.

She is asking them to squint up at facts and figures, graphs and slides and to take in material in a way that they are not physically equipped to do. This is material she could easily share with them online, or give out later on a cheat sheet. And all the while she is missing the opportunity of the presentation to win hearts and minds and get some real reaction.

We have all heard poor speakers, and have completely zoned out while they are on the platform, wishing we had not sat so close to the front where it was impossible to slip out unnoticed! Actually, we are quite selfish as listeners. We want to know straight away what is in this for me?

The things that make us zone out are usually:

- **Irrelevancy** – This talk is not addressing me or my needs
- **Boredom** – I can't stay focused
- **Complexity** – I can't follow what he is on about
- **Density** – Too much material
- **No examples** – I don't get it
- **Monotone delivery** – Her tone is sending me to sleep
- **Connection missing** – He is not reaching out to me

- **Credibility lack** – She has not made it clear why I should listen
- **Discomfort** – I don't like his obvious unease
- **Personality missing** – I can't get a sense of who she is

Good speakers, on the other hand, speak to you as if you are the only person in the room. They use conversational language, which is easy to listen to and easy to understand. They capture your attention immediately, and hold it throughout the talk. They look and sound relaxed and in control.

The talk is colourful, interesting and informative. When it comes to the end, you realise it had a structure and a purpose to it, and you experience a feeling of satisfaction.

In very simple terms, most good talks follow the same pattern. They have a big opening, a number of clear messages, which are illustrated well, and a big closing. The closing may in some way circle back to the opening, which adds to that notion of satisfaction.

If you were to draw a diagram for a good talk, it would look like this:

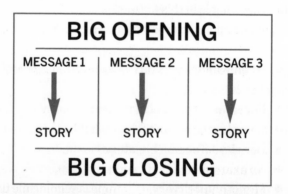

The Big Opening is where you jump straight in with a story, an unusual or intriguing fact, some drama, a question, a demand – anything but housekeeping.

The idea is to catch the attention immediately and make them think, this is going to be good, I'm really glad I came in to this session.

Comedians often start with the line, "A funny thing happened on the way in to the theatre tonight." Of course we know it didn't happen that day, but we enjoy the immediacy and the sense of a story about to begin so we pay attention.

Then the talk goes on to its key messages, each one illustrated with an anecdote or a story.

And it finishes up with a Big Closing, often something visionary or uplifting, which gets the audience thinking about the future, and how things will be from now on.

We often describe the prepared closing in a talk as a Parachute. It is the place you go to when the chairperson of the event tinkles the glass to tell you to wrap up, and you take a minute or two to finish up strongly. You have your parachute ready, it opens up, and allows you to land well. You don't panic, when you come to the end of your time, and stop dead.

There is nothing worse at the end of a talk than a lame fade out, the speaker saying, "So, em, I think... em... that's where I'll finish up... em... maybe... em..." Pause.

And then a hopeful, "I wonder are there any questions?"

Or the other scenario where the speaker has three or four endings, one after the other, and the audience begins to get very restless and uncomfortable.

Attending a conference recently, where one of the speakers was clearly reading out a script, I saw the Chair signal to her that her time was up. She nodded, but kept on reading.

She read another full page, and turned another page, and another one, and another one, completely ignoring the now frantic signals from the Chair. The audience was at this stage coughing, shifting in the seats, sighing, checking mobile phones and showing all the usual signs that they are losing the will to live.

The speaker clearly had no interest in the comfort of her audience, and no ability to summarise what she was about, or to go to a good strong closing when her agreed time was up. It is unprofessional, and it is also inconsiderate to the event organisers and the other speakers.

Good speakers are deeply concerned about their audience. In fact they know that the audience always comes first, regardless of the type of talk or presentation to be made.

Preparing the Talk

So here it is, the ten-step, three-phase approach to the perfect presentation, the one that will allow you to shine as a performing leader.

The Thinking Phase –
Audience, Goal and Message

1. Audience

Where do you do your best thinking? In the bath? On the treadmill? Walking the dog? Driving home in the evening? Wherever it is, that is the place where your talk begins to emerge, your ideas start to take shape, and your objectives begin to become clear.

A good talk starts with the audience, not with the list of things you want to say. In the corporate world, people often have difficulty with this one.

I hear people saying all the time, "Oh but I have to present the results", or "I have to outline the plans for the coming year", or "I have to tell them all about the sales drive." Of course you do, but you have to tell it in a way that is relevant and interesting to them, or you may as well save yourself the bother, because they will just drift off while you are speaking.

You start by really thinking about your audience, and asking yourself who exactly are they, why will they be there on the day and what will their expectations be? Although you will be the person on the platform, in the spotlight, they are actually the important people in the room, not you. You are just the conduit for the message.

So you research your audience and what they might already know about the topic, or what they still need to find out. You also need to get a handle on what they know about you as the speaker or presenter of the subject, and what they perceive your expertise to be.

You need to establish whether the audience is more less coming from the one place, or whether it comprises different interest groups and stakeholders, in which case your message will have to impact on a few different levels.

> *Tip: What is the hook that will grab this audience, unite them and engage them to really listen to the message.*

2. Message

Now think about the message or messages you want to get across. This is often quite clear in the case of company targets and objectives, but a bit more obscure when you are dreaming up a topic for that TED talk. Or when you are trying to think of a way of engaging an audience with your social enterprise so they will become involved, or contribute in some way.

Your messages should be distinct and clear, and when planning them, you should keep reminding yourself that less is more. Better that your audience take on board one clear thought that they fully understand and act upon, rather than hearing loads of facts that have no impact at all.

> *Tip: With messaging, less is more*

3. Goal

You then have to ask yourself, what do you want this audience to do as a result of listening to you, and hearing these messages. That is your goal.

Do you want them to be motivated, or inspired, or entertained? To hire you or to buy your product? To be enlightened or informed? To become an advocate for a cause or spread a message?

So by the end of your thinking phase, you should have worked out how your messages at point 2 will be designed so that the audience at point 1 will allow you to achieve your goal at point 3.

Tip: Be clear on the goal of your presentation

And now you know what you want to achieve, so you are ready to start mapping out your presentation.

The Preparing Phase – Mapping, Blocking, Linking, Re-sequencing
4. Mapping

So how do you start putting your thoughts on paper?

You can use a mind map, dumping all your thoughts and ideas on a big sheet, with boxes and charts and clouds and arrows going everywhere. You can scribble a few thoughts on the back of a beer mat. You can open the laptop and type furiously, getting it all out of your head and onto the screen. You can knock yourself out with bullet points. You can write it out in longhand.

It doesn't actually matter at all which method you choose, once you assemble the information somewhere, to see what you have got. Research comes into play here, allowing you to support your information with facts.

Tip: Capture your thoughts in the way that works for you

5. Blocking

Now you have to get the thoughts corralled into themes and logical blocks of information, starting work on the examples and illustrations you will use to make each block come alive.

This is really important. You have to have a very clear idea of how you are going to get each idea across. That means the actual story, anecdote or description you will use which will not only make your material really interesting for the audience, but it will also help you remember it.

> *Tip: Decide on your blocks, and match each one with a good example of what you are talking about, something you have experienced personally.*

6. Linking

In delivering a speech, people rarely get lost in the blocks, particularly if they have a good story attached. But they can get confused in the links. Good talks flow smoothly from one idea to the next, the links connecting the blocks in a natural way.

Think about your links, the couple of sentences that will connect the last idea to the next one smoothly. This is what a continuity announcer does on television, or a DJ does on the radio. They take us seamlessly from one programme or song to the next one, somehow connecting them in our minds.

Links are all about Content, Context and Continuity.

> *Tip: You will know you have your links right when they make your talk flow smoothly.*

7. Re-sequencing

You may find that certain blocks, no matter how you link them, don't flow into one another. So change the blocks around. Play with them until you are happy that you have found ways of getting them to connect up in several different ways.

This is where a lot of people get their talk preparation wrong. When we write, we usually follow a logical sequence, and assume that we have to deliver the talk in this sequence. But actually we don't. No one in the audience knows how you originally mapped things out, and it may work better in a different way.

David Bowie says the lyrics from some of his best songs resulted from experimenting with chopped up sentences and rearranged lines. In the same way, you may need to move the furniture about, to give your room a different look!

Tip: You can give yourself great comfort in knowing that your blocks work equally well in several different ways.

The Practising Phase – Headings, Vocalising, Visualising
8. Headings

After you have reconstructed your talk, and are really happy that your blocks are a moveable feast, think of headings that will identify each block. The heading should be a meaningful idea. It should refer to the illustration of the message, and not to an abstract point.

It is possible to give a great twenty minute talk with no notes at all other than a few headings on a prompt card or on your iPad but the headings have to be meaningful. If your heading is 'marketing' or 'financials', there is a danger that in the heat of the moment you might not remember what you were going to say.

Much better to have a heading that prompts you to tell the story about Mike's great marketing drive in Cork last year, or a heading that suggests you describe how the big sale in Belfast was won, or even the punchline to a good story.

Tip: Choose meaningful headings for your prompts.

9. Vocalising

Saying chunks of the talk out loud is very important. Driving home in the evening, or on that treadmill again, you need to hear yourself trying out the stories you will tell, so you can refine them, and avoid rambling.

But it is equally important not to give the whole talk too often from start to finish, or you will start learning off pieces, and begin to put yourself into the learned memory zone, rather than keeping the talk in personal memory.

Over-rehearsing, or learning things off by heart, causes a speaker to come across as scripted and false. The best speakers work really hard to sound natural and spontaneous.

> *Tip: When vocalising your blocks to hear how they sound, do them singly and not in order.*

10. Visualising

I think it is obvious at this stage that you should promise yourself that you will never, ever again start a presentation by opening up your laptop and going to slide one! Starting there is shooting yourself in the foot, locking yourself into a linear presentation that prevents you from giving of your best.

But if at this point of your talk preparation, it is clear that some concepts need something else to connect with the audience, then you think about a visual – a picture or illustration that will bring the point home, or make the audience smile, or even wonder what this is about.

Death by PowerPoint is one of the curses of modern business life. Slides should only ever be used when they serve a genuine purpose – to enhance the communication. Unfortunately they are used every day all over the world for no reason at all except that people mistakenly think they will look unprepared if they show up without them.

Tip: Ask yourself is the slide there for you, as a personal prompt, or is it there for the audience?

Preparing yourself

Doing the work, as described above, puts you in a great place to tackle a talk. You are setting yourself up for success by using a system that frees you up to showcase the best version of yourself, not a machine who looks and sounds like he swallowed the corporate manual before he went up on stage.

The best version of yourself is the person you really are – the person your friends and family see every day. There is no better version of you. That's it. That's the one.

It's fully honest, and if you are honest you will know that the smiles, applause and any other affirmation you get is fully deserved. It is for the real you.

I describe it as 'wearing the bus driver's hat' when someone presents in a way they think is expected of them, rather than in a way that is true to themselves. They think that when representing the company or the organisation they need to look and sound and act like the bus driver. So they plant the hat firmly on their heads and tie up their communication in language they never normally use.

The alternative is to be yourself, to focus so strongly on meeting the needs of the audience and on delivering understandable messages, that your true self shines out, and your enthusiasm and passion for the subject lights up the room.

This is authentic presentation, the best kind of public speaking possible.

I need to know you if I am going to listen to you, and if I am going to do what you ask of me. And the only way I can know you, as a speaker, is if I can see you. So you have to have the confidence to let me see you.

You let me see you by sharing some detail about yourself as you speak but, and this is a really big but, that is not to be confused with talking about yourself.

You use yourself to make a point, to share an insight, to show that it is just the same for you, but not to brag, or big yourself up, or try to impress.

I have listened to many talks from people on the business speaking circuit who have misunderstood this. They are asked to speak at Chamber of Commerce or Women in Business events to share their story, and they think that this is an open invitation to talk about themselves for an hour.

"I went to college in... and then I went to America for a few years... And then I came home and set up my business... And I have been hugely successful... And I think it is easy to do and anyone can do it..." Blah, blah, blah!

As a listener, the only thing going through your mind as they ramble on is, "And your point is?"

What is happening is that the speaker is getting bogged down with information, while the audience is looking for insight.

An experienced speaker understands that when you are invited to come to an event to share your story, you are really being asked to use yourself as a means to show what you have learned along the way. What are the things you would do differently if you had your time again, for example.

You give vignettes from your own story to show experience and empathy, and to build a bridge across which the audience can travel, but that is definitely not to be confused with self indulgence!

And the best speakers are always looking to improve, to raise their personal bar. They never sit back and convince themselves that they have this thing cracked, and they don't need to work on it any more. After every single outing, they choose someone they respect to give them honest feedback.

The Panel Discussion

Have you noticed that panel discussions have become really popular at conferences? Event planners and conference organisers are clearly reacting to bad speakers and death by PowerPoint and are working hard to make these occasions more enjoyable for all of us.

So after the opening address and the first keynote from the podium, you will usually find an armchair setting with an MC or Moderator to introduce a panel of speakers and to field some questions.

For those planning seminars and kick-offs, it is a great way of changing the pace and tone, breaking up the main presentations and getting more people onto the platform. This varies the voices and the points of view, and of course gets good questions and interactivity from the audience.

For speakers, it is a great opportunity to take part in an event in a less pressurised way than delivering a thirty- or forty-minute speech. The only disadvantage to it is that you have a much shorter time to get your message out.

And there may also be someone who is an industry expert but an inexperienced Chair in the moderator role, and they can allow one speaker to dominate, or fail to keep the topics moving along.

When you agree to take part in a panel, you take your chances!

Depending on the format, each panellist can be asked to make a short stand-alone presentation, followed by the question and answer session. Or sometimes the whole panel discussion is simply a series of questions and answers, with no overview piece beforehand.

So if the panel segment is running from 10am to 11am, and each panellist has been asked to speak for about 6 minutes first, the Moderator's running order will look something like this:

10.00	Introduction of topic and speakers.
	Call first speaker
10.03	Speaker 1
10.10	Introduce Speaker 2
10.12	Speaker 2
10.20	Introduce Speaker 3
10.22	Speaker 3
10.30	Introduce Speaker 4
10.32	Speaker 4
10.40	Begin Q & A
10.58	Wrap Up

You can see how tight it is, and how the Moderator will have to work really hard to get everyone started and finished promptly, so that there will be time left for the Q & A, and the all important audience involvement.

In a six-minute talk, allowing a minute or two of grace as we have set out above, you will really only get across one or maybe two messages. Better to say one or two things that will resonate and be remembered, rather than running through a list of things that will be forgotten immediately you leave the stage.

So you should use the same format described earlier as regards the big opening and the big closing, but confine yourself to a lot less material in the middle.

The clock is everything in a panel discussion. Take your mobile with you, on silent, place it on the podium beside you, use the stop watch, and finish up within a minute of your time – simple professionalism and courtesy.

The presentation part out of the way, you then have to think about the Q & A, and how you can use the opportunity to reinforce some messaging from your talk, or to make some new points that were not covered.

I was working recently with the leadership team in a major tech firm who had decided that the previous year's annual conference had been a bit dull so they wanted to do something different this year.

They told me that previously they each had to present to the audience of 1,000 people a short piece on their area of responsibility, something they were very familiar with, and which should not have been a problem. However, the event team had micromanaged the whole day, and the speakers had felt over-scripted, locked in to set-piece contributions, and very awkward to the point of having their credibility undermined in front of the business.

They were determined not to let the same thing happen again.

So we decided that this year the session with the team leaders should be a panel discussion, with a TV personality as MC. We worked on simplifying their messages down to a vision for what each department could achieve, an expression of belief in the team to deliver the vision, and a couple of specific asks from the leader so that the vision could start rolling out.

That gave a structure and an intent to every response the leader would make, regardless of where the TV presenter might find inspiration for his question, or where he might decide to take the conversation.

Then we began working on key messages which each leader would build in to his or her replies, and a story or illustration to match each message to show how this would benefit the team and make their work easier.

The last thing was agreeing that no one would use notes, so that the leaders would really listen to the questions and the whole conversation, so they could support each other if necessary and keep the session sounding very casual and informal, despite the strong messages that were to be delivered.

Afterwards, I heard that it had gone very well. The team said they had really enjoyed the occasion, done the job well and, more importantly, that they had come across as themselves.

A panel discussion, like the one described here, is a bit like doing a media interview. The questions can come from anywhere, and you have to be prepared to tackle the issue in hand, while moving it on to one of your key messages.

A good way to think about it is to remember that each of your answers is supposed to aid the understanding of the audience. So use the word AID to remind you to:

Address
Illustrate
Direct

Address the issue you have been asked about. That is slightly different to trying to answer the question, which you may not be able to do, if you don't have the facts to hand. You can always offer to find the facts and send them on later, but in the meantime you have a great opportunity to address the issue, bringing insight that otherwise might not have been thought about by anyone there, and to skilfully start bringing your contribution around to one of your messages.

Illustrate what you mean. Share an anecdote or find a good analogy to introduce colour and description to what are you saying, which immediately makes the message completely understandable to the audience and anchors it in their minds. If your anecdote is good enough, this is what they will be talking about at the coffee break, your message having gone home, straight and true.

Direct the end of your answer to another one of your messages, using key words to place a hook in the mix for the Moderator to pick up on. By that I mean as you finish off your answer, say something like, "That's why people always wonder where we source the products, and how we get them here on time".

It absolutely begs the question, well where do you source the products, and how do the logistics work?

Using the AID system of answering does a few things.

It takes the fear out of any question that might be thrown at you. You will not be stuck, you have a system to use and will always be able to give a credible answer.

It also allows you to really focus on what is going on, in the moment, and to be fully mindful of what your fellow panellists are saying, rather than shutting them out so you can rehearse your own answer! You look stronger as a panellist when you are able to refer to something your colleague has just said, and build on it within your own answer.

So a panel discussion is not a solo run. It is a joint contribution, and to my mind you should act like you remember that while you are on the platform. Or you might not get asked back.

♦   ♦   ♦

Speaking in public is a great privilege and a great honor, and should be treated as such. Bill Clinton had a very public lesson on how not to do it early in his career.

In 1988, as Governor of Arkansas, he was invited by his friend Democratic Presidential candidate Mike Dukakis to be the warm up act at the national convention. Clinton wasted the great opportunity to shine as a leader by relying on a script, which obviously had no relevance to the audience.

The more he tried to engage with the poor material, the more the audience ignored him, waved their placards, and turned their backs on him – all captured on camera and gleefully relayed to the nation by the TV presenters. The only real reaction Clinton got was when he began to say, "In closing...." when the audience cheered loudly, delighted he was finished.

Mortifying for a politician, but he learned from the experience, and became a hugely impressive speaker.

Most of us will never reach the heights of a JFK, or a Martin Luther King who undoubtedly had the benefit of brilliant speech writers, but who were themselves the very definition of performing leaders.

They not only put the audience first, planned great messages, gave brilliant examples, showed their vulnerability, and were fully authentic – but they understood rhythm and timing. And they were able to perform and deliver to a very high level the constructs the speech writers worked in.

Typical constructs are phrases of three – left, right and centre; the good the bad and the ugly; on the beaches, on the streets and in the air – or phrases of opposites – to be or not to be; on the one hand or on the other; when the going gets tough, the tough get going.

That last one originated from Pierre Salinger, speech writer for Bobby Kennedy, not Billy Ocean, as many people seem to think!

Working musicality and cadence of this level into your speech is premiership stuff, and perhaps beyond the reach of a lot of us, but it is a fascinating subject, and well worth reading up on.

Why not try out one in your next speech and see how it sounds?

TED and TEDx

TED talks have been around for 25 years now, but the 'ideas worth spreading' concept, to which the movement is devoted, has taken off wildly in the past decade or so with talks shared again and again online.

The licensing of the brand as TEDx to universities, businesses and community groups all over the world means that giving a talk yourself is now quite achievable, as there are now so many events run, and it is well worth ticking off the bucket list.

You usually have to upload a one or two minute video of yourself outlining your 'idea worth spreading', so the organisers can get a sense of who you are and how you perform. Then they choose their line-up for the day based firstly on solid ideas, but also with a view to including people who offer different backgrounds and experiences.

But it is nerve wracking, I can't pretend otherwise!

A couple of years ago, just before I did a talk at TEDx Tallaght, I had been spending some time with a great young man, a school friend of my sons', Jack Kavanagh. Jack broke his neck, at age 20, diving into a wave and had been left paralysed from the chest down.

I met him to give him some help with media interviews and was struck by his extraordinary attitude. By some incredible gift of mental strength, and the support of a brilliant family and community, just one year on from his accident he was adjusting to what had happened to him.

I thought he was a brilliant example for young people and got his permission to refer to him in my talk.

But on the red mat, hit by the impact of the TED occasion, and seeing the faces of my own lads in the audience, I developed a serious wobble in my voice when speaking about Jack.

But here is the great part of the story, the part where you could say the circle was squared.

I was invited by TEDx Tallaght to come back and MC the following year's event, along with speaker coach Padraig Hyland, and to do some work with the speakers.

I had the enormous pleasure of introducing onto the red mat Jack Kavanagh, taking his place as a TEDx speaker at only 22 years of age, and I am thrilled to say, knocking it right out of the park.

He has since registered with Frankie Sheahan's Front Row speaker's agency, so you know where to go if you want to find a great motivational speaker for your next event!

Chapter Four

Performing On The Media

In this chapter you will get the lowdown on how to prepare for and deliver a really good media interview, and you'll learn about the pitfalls to avoid. Journalists aren't out to get you. Genuinely! They are out to get the story, and to get the story out.

♦   ♦   ♦

"AND we're live".

Those are the words from the floor manager as the red light comes on, the presenter looks to camera, and the moment you have been waiting for – with either dread or anticipation – is here. You are about to speak to the nation, and it is going to work out really well, or then again maybe it isn't.

You are a guest on the TV programme this evening to defend your company or personal reputation, or perhaps as an 'expert' to give your views on entrepreneurship or the economy; or maybe as a spokesperson for a cause or concern. Either way, tomorrow morning you will do one of two things.

You will sail out your front door, delighted with yourself. You'll head to work with a smile on your face, and stroll like a master of the universe out of the lift and through the department, basking in the glow of congratulation and pats on the back.

Or you will sprint to the car, dodging the knowing look from Johnny across the street, and use the fire escape to creep into your office, to barricade yourself behind a pile of reports and deadlines and avoid the canteen at lunchtime.

A media outing is a huge opportunity. Well prepared, and with a good insight to how the game is played, you can and will do very well. But it is also a minefield, and careers can be ended with very public mistakes by those who wing it, or who take on more than they can handle.

If you are going to be the spokesperson for your company or organisation, and you will be appearing on a prime time show, do yourself a big favour and get some training from any one of the professionals out there who do a great job!

You wouldn't buy a business without getting advice from a lawyer or an accountant, or run a marathon without working with a fitness coach. So don't chance doing a major outing without good support. But in the meantime, there are plenty of things you can learn here, which will give you insight to how the media works in practice, and which are useful skills for local interviews and less pressurised occasions.

When we work with people preparing for the media, we start by recording a practice interview. Straight away people can see what they are doing wrong.

In a recent group:

- Aisling said she didn't say what she wanted to say at all. She got steered into talking about a former role rather than talking about her current business, which was what she was there to do.

- Dorothea was concerned about using lots of words to say nothing, and over-using words such as 'like' and 'basically'. She gets a bit nervous about her use of English, as it is not her first language.
- Patrick said he felt really self-conscious and that he had been ambushed. He said the style of interview had been very interrogatory.
- Lynn thought she had been waffling. She had been waiting for lots of tough questions, so she carried on talking about nothing waiting for an interjection. When the question came, it was from a completely different place, and she waffled again.
- Marie felt she didn't explain herself at all. She is used to talking to people who already know about the subject, and found it hard to explain the basics to a new audience.
- Avril felt she had been led down a road, fell into traps, and got very defensive. She got flustered and then couldn't collect her thoughts as well as she normally does.
- Michael thought he had come across as a know it all. He said nervousness had made him a bit aggressive.
- Arthur said that he felt like punching the interviewer throughout the encounter, and wasted the whole time looking for retribution!

Actually, none of these first interviews were half as bad as the people themselves thought. Some of them were really quite good, with the interviewees sounding authoritative and knowledgeable, despite making the mistakes they ably spotted themselves.

Media starts to become easy once you understand the rules of engagement, and once you get in some practice. A lot of it is common sense, and the kind of stuff you know already. And once you start thinking about this, you will start listening to media interviews in a new way, and training your ear to spot what works and what doesn't.

Try this one out.

The next time you are listening to your favourite radio station driving in your car, or sitting in your kitchen, pick an interview and listen to it closely from start to finish. It will probably be six or seven minutes long.

Now turn down the sound, really think about the interview, and ask yourself a few questions. What was the one single message that jumped out at you from this interview? How was that message illustrated? Was the interview interesting? Did you believe the spokesperson?

Your answers to those questions tell you straight away was this a good interviewee or not. If you have no idea what he was talking about, he wasted his time going into the studio that day.

If he spoke in an abstract way, and didn't give you a memorable picture to take away with you, he was wasting his time. If he bored you, he definitely should have stayed in bed that morning. And if you didn't believe him, well, what can we say?

When it is your turn to do an interview, you want to aim for:

Clarity
Credibility
Colour

Listening at home, or in my car, I want to be very clear about what you are saying to me. I want to hear in your voice and your conviction that you are genuine and therefore I will warm to you and believe in you. And I want to hear your thoughts presented in a colourful way that will resonate with me, and make me remember exactly what it was you said.

And this gives you the water cooler moment, the thing that people will be talking about later in the day.

Siobhan Talbot, the CEO of dairy giant Glanbia, did an interview with one of the main early morning radio chat shows for International Women's Day and later I overheard this conversation.

"Did you hear your woman on this morning, wasn't she amazing? She is running one of the biggest businesses in the country, and she makes it sound so easy. And she had cancer a couple of years ago."

"Yeah, and she has kids and everything, and she sounds so nice. She comes across as really warm and friendly."

"She should be running the country. Maybe she would think of going for politics."

I think they liked her!

Doing a good interview is about getting your ducks in a row beforehand, knowing how to prepare without over preparing, and knowing the rules of engagement.

It is about realising that you are not at the complete mercy of the interviewer, as comfortable in the studio as he is in his own living room. There are plenty of things you can do to get some control, and to steer the interview to where you want it to go.

Here are a few ideas for you to think about:

An interview is not an exam

Yes you are the Principal of the college, or the Head of Marketing, or the CEO of the firm, but even with the title and all the responsibility that goes with it, you are not expected to know everything. If you crowd your head with all the facts and figures beforehand, terrified that you will be caught out, you will not be 'in the moment' in studio, or mindful enough to make the most of the opportunity.

The interviewer is not an examiner and she is not testing you.

All she is doing is trying to make you interesting to keep her listeners tuned in, or keep her readers going to the end of the article.

Journalists are not out to get you. They are out to get the story. Genuinely!

So if you are honest, interesting and engaging, they won't have to get out the spade and start digging, nor will they become argumentative or difficult. You will have made their job easier by giving up good solid material that is interesting for the listener, viewer or reader.

The alternative is to be flat, boring and evasive, and then to have the interest extracted out of you by a clever, probing journalist, in much the way as a dentist uses those noisy instruments. The choice is yours!

Answering the First Question

Your opening answer is probably the most important part of the whole interview. It is a big opportunity for you to set out your stall, and to drop in some key words and ideas that the interviewer may come back to as the interview progresses.

Interviewers expect this, and can get caught out if you are too abrupt.

Once when I was doing some stand-in presenting on my local station a spokesperson for a hospital support group was the interviewee. I started by asking him how the campaign was going, and he said fine.

And then he stopped. And waited.

I nearly fell off my chair!

I had just been reading my running order to see how long this interview should last, and listening at the same time on talk-back to my producer telling me that we'd be taking an unscheduled ad break, and would I like my coffee sent in?

This is actually quite normal. There is a bit of housekeeping going on at the start of an interview, particularly on radio, and it gives a well prepared interviewee a bit of a 'free run'. This is a chance to set the tone for the whole exchange, particularly if you get a 'soft' first question like the one I proffered.

But you shouldn't ever count on a straightforward 'how is the project going' type of opening question.

A first question is a ball that can be lobbed in from absolutely anywhere in the field, and you have to be ready for it. Some people never get over the shock of the randomness of the first question, and are then on the back foot for the rest of the interview.

So listen well, answer the question you are asked, and *go on to lay out the parameters of what you are there to talk about*, taking your time to do it, and making sure there is an interesting hook or two in the mix.

Inexperienced interviewees will give an opening answer that lasts for maybe 19 or 20 seconds – or two seconds flat if they are like my hospital friend. Listen out over the next few days and you will begin to spot them.

The old hands will speak for well over a minute, benefitting from a kind of unwritten convention that this is a polite amount of time for a first answer.

And sometimes also benefitting from the distraction of the programme host!

Getting into the Driving Seat

So who has their hands on the wheel during an interview? It can be you, if you know how to go about it.

Larger than life Irish Government Minister, Padraig Flynn, known as Pee Flynn, was notorious for answering journalists questions with the words "I'm glad you asked me that", and then proceeding to go off on a tangent of his own that completely ignored the question.

The problem with ignoring the question is that the journalist wants to know why, and will go after the answer relentlessly.

You will no doubt have heard of the famous Jeremy Paxman interview on Newsnight when he asked the UK Home Secretary Michael Howard the same question 14 times in a row.

He kept Howard wriggling and squirming for ages, in what has now become one of those famous clips that is played over and over again on YouTube.

So, to avoid this, it is a good idea, a really good idea, to answer the question you are asked.

Taking over the driving seat in an interview is not about avoiding questions, it is about answering them. And answering them so well and in such an interesting way, that you can roll seamlessly on to wherever you want to go next.

The interviewer, happy with the original answer, and the quality of your information, may well be inclined to go along with you. It is that simple.

But:

- If you don't know the answer – say so.
- If you know the answer, but haven't the authority to divulge the information – say so.
- If you don't want to answer – say so. (There is no law that says you have to!)

It is ignoring the question, or studiously avoiding it, that causes the problem, and leads to the kind of antics that are mind-numbingly irritating for those of us listening at home.

Controlling Tempo, Tone, and Tension

As the interview progresses, you retain control by answering the questions you are asked, and continuing on to a point you want to make. You plan these points before you go into the studio. And to use a sporting analogy, you have to think of each exchange as playing soccer and not table tennis.

In table tennis, the ball is going pit pat, pit pat, back and forward across the table. In soccer, you get that ball, retain possession, withstand tackles, dribble it all the way up the pitch, aim for goal, and score. That is what each of your answers should look and feel like.

How the answers sound is very dependent on how well you control tempo, tone and tension, and I have to put my hand up here and say I am a fine one to talk. As a guest in studio, as opposed to a presenter, this is something I often get wrong.

My enthusiasm for the subject, and my urgency to get it across in the short time available, means that I sometimes speak too fast, and allow my voice to rise. But if I explain it to you here, hopefully you will do a better job when your turn comes. Don't do as I do, do as I say!

Tempo: When the pace is steady and controlled, you keep your thoughts in order and get your ideas out coherently, and in complete sentences rather than in broken phrases. When the distance between the question and answer keeps shortening, hearts beat faster, palms become sweaty, anxiety creeps in, and voices go shrill.

Controlling the tempo is about playing soccer, as described above, and not being afraid to use short pauses and reflection in answering.

Tone: Finding the right voice will influence the tempo. As a guest on a programme, your job is to sound conversational, explanatory, knowledgeable, expert. And to find the kind of language that gives you the space to expand.

Phrases that work well are: "Let me explain what I mean by that" or "To put that another way..." or "There are a couple of important points about that which I think are worth sharing..."

Tension: It is much harder for hostility or aggression to enter the frame when the tone and tempo are being controlled. It takes two to tango, and an interviewer can't possibly have a row with himself.

He can always try the adversarial approach to the interview, and is quite within his rights to do so, but if you do not mirror his tone or tempo, and stay in your own zone, you'll be fine.

You have to do your swan impersonation! Stay cool and calm on top and do all the paddling underneath.

Putting interest into the interview

The media is a very crowded space with more competition than ever, and we are spoiled for choice by the number of radio and TV stations we have access to. This makes us very fickle.

Just one irritating guest or poor song choice, and we change station or channel hop until we are happy.

Those of us who still read newspapers have the same pull on our attention span. If the article we are reading is not holding our attention, we throw the paper on the sofa, and pick up our iPads to start Tweeting or Facebooking instead.

So we have to make interviews interesting and we do it with

> **Pictures**
> **Passion**
> **Persuasion**

Pictures: I remember seeing an interview once on a heritage programme where this very elderly farmer sitting in his kitchen in a remote location on the side of a mountain was being asked about using modern technology. He said he preferred the radio to the television because the pictures were better!

He was clearly listening to good radio, where his imagination was being stimulated to colour the scene.

When you are being interviewed for radio, TV, print or online, the more pictures, stories and examples you can provide, the better the outcome will be. That's because they go straight to the reader or the listener and make them feel part of your world.

You connect with the audience by putting a picture in their head of what you are talking about and making them care about it, describing in the here and now what is going on, rather than speaking in an abstract way.

This is perhaps why the 'sick child' slot, as people in the industry refer to it, has become so popular on chat shows. Regardless of how jaded or cynical we are, when we listen to a couple describe very personally, and usually very emotionally, what is happening with their child's situation, we become completely involved.

Although we are listening to their story, we are relating it back to our own lives and thinking about relatives or friends going through the same thing. Through personal and intimate story telling, they are building a bridge which we cross over.

And yes, in communication terms, the task is a lot harder when it is a business situation you are describing. How do you create a picture, and add in feeling to make it connect?

You do it by getting to "the other day I met a man..." as quickly as possible, a real example of how the product or service or idea works in action. Because the story you tell will make the point far more efficiently and memorably than anything you can do in the abstract.

US President Ronald Regan, an acknowledged expert leadership performer and communicator, used to say that if he had not got to Bill and Joan within seventeen seconds, the interview was not going well. He meant that he had to bring the message straight to the ordinary man and woman on the street, or he knew people would tune out.

Interviewers know that this is what you are doing, but they can't help themselves. They are seduced by the power of the story too. And they find it hard to interrupt, knowing that this is what the listener and the reader want.

MEP Mairéad McGuinness was being interviewed during the last European Elections one morning when, as a former journalist herself, and indeed a gifted communicator, she answered the point and went straight into a story. "Out campaigning last Wednesday I met a man who said..."

The interviewer, clearly anxious to show that there are no flies on him, came right back with "Oh, come on Mairéad, so you are going to start into I met a man, this better be good."

But then he sat right back in the chair and let her off! She got a clear run at the next few minutes of airtime.

It was as if the interviewer, having clearly signalled that he knew what she was up to, was satisfied at that, and had no further need to interrupt. So he let her finish that story, and roll right on to make two or three more really good points. Game set and match to Mairéad.

Passion: We can't fake interest or knowledge in a subject. We either care about something or we don't. And the only subjects we should ever talk about publicly are those we do actually care about.

Because it is this concern that gives us direction and fluency, and a degree of protection. If you are speaking passionately about something you really believe in, no matter where an interviewer or fellow panellist stands on the issue, a part of them has to respect your beliefs.

I have a friend who has become a panellist and commentator quite recently, having retrained in journalism after a very different career. She is really good at it, and makes it her business to stay on top of any subject on which she might be asked to give a view.

But she told me recently about her sense of panic when she knows a topic is coming up which she hasn't covered before. She rings her sister and asks her, "What do I think about the proposed tax hike?"

It is not that she is actually asking the sister to spoon-feed her some views. She is using the sounding board of a trusted family member to vocalise her views before she goes on air; to bounce them around, hear how they sound – out loud – and get her thoughts aligned before that red light goes on.

It's good practice, because when she is in studio she now has ownership of the ideas and they come across confidently and well.

We like listening to enthusiasm, and we like listening to expertise. We like listening to an enthusiastic expert most of all.

Entrepreneurs are often criticised for the casual way they use the word 'passion'. They are passionate about start-ups, and widgets, and the App that is going to change the world, and the international cleaning business, or whatever it is that they are working on at the moment.

But they are not lying. They usually are seriously into those things. They have to be, to withstand the pressures of staying with a single product or concept all the way. So they become very focused. The good ones have a way of making that one thing very interesting, and talking about it in a way that engages us and makes us want to know more.

Persuasion: We are quite selfish in the way we listen, view and read. We scan things for their relevance to our own lives and worlds. A good interviewee knows this and is always thinking about the audience and putting them first.

I call it finding your Touchstone Tom. Who is your ideal listener or reader? The person you really want to convince today during this interview that this is a good product, or service or idea. Is it a potential investor, a customer, a politician, a stake-holder?

Whoever it is, and make it a real person, not an imaginary one, he is who you should be talking to throughout the interview, in the kind of direct language that will capture him and convince him.

If you met him at a function, or in the street, how would you explain the concept to him and win him around? That is what you have to do on air, avoiding the trap of over engaging with the interviewer, as if he or she is the end goal, and not the conduit to the audience.

Preparing your messages for any interview should start with the audience, the demographic for that particular program or publication. That is the 'what' piece, the one or two key things you are going to get across today.

And then you have to plan the 'how' – the stories and examples you will use, as described earlier, to get those messages across, and persuade the listener to agree with you.

Removing the Bus Driver's Hat

What is it about walking into a radio or TV studio, or sitting down in front of a journalist with a recording device on the table, that makes a lot of people take out the bus driver's hat and plonk it firmly on their head, in a similar way to the corporate presenter, mentioned earlier?

By that I mean that as they are now the official public representative of the company or the concern, they think they should speak in a formal, stilted way. They become very grand, very complex, use convoluted explanations, and the whole purpose of the communication goes out the window.

People who do this are actually afraid. They are hiding behind the hat, and the uniform, thinking that this is safe. It will impress the folks back in the office, and will sound very professional and highbrow.

It actually does the opposite. It makes everything too abstract to hold our interest, so we zone out, or change the channel.

Have you ever been driving in traffic with the radio on, listening to a business programme and there is some chap banging on about his metrics, and his quarter four projections, and his knowledge process outsourcing, and so on. And you find yourself wondering what's on the telly tonight, or if your partner remembered to bring the dog to the vet?

He is boring so your thoughts ramble.

But the next guest starts with: "Wait till I tell about this great little thing we did which increased our turnover by 30% last year. The company is flying now and it all began when..."

And what do you do? You lean in and turn up the sound, thinking: "I could do with some of that. I need to listen to this one".

The second guest is speaking normally and enthusiastically and is about to share a story about something real and understandable that is of complete interest to you and your world, so you pay attention.

Having the confidence to let go of formality and jargon and let your personality out of the bag, gives you the best chance of doing the kind of interview that connects.

And don't ever worry about your accent, your ums and your aahs and your personal mannerisms. These only become irritating if you have nothing to say. Forget about fishing for a bigger word to impress your mother. Just say what you have to say in a way that connects with us, and we won't notice your personal tics.

Managing Time

Time in an 'on air' studio has a special quality. It goes twice as fast as normal time. Not literally, but it feels that way.

You will usually be told, as a guest on a show, roughly how long the interview will run. So you will hear that they are taking you after the last ad break and before the news, and that it's a 5 or 6 minute slot; or they might say they will be coming to you at the top of the program, and you'll be getting about 15 minutes.

You prepare accordingly, and then it all changes. Because a Government Minister is suddenly available to talk about the interest rate hikes, and the presenter is told to finish up with you. Right now. Or even more scarily, the Jeremy Paxman scenario, where the Minister can't come into studio after all and the producer says: "Keep this interview going for another 10 minutes"!

So it is a moveable feast, and you have no idea where it is moving to next.

You manage the time by keeping your answers succinct. Remember the soccer analogy? It is very obvious when your response has scored a goal, and therefore it is very easy to stop there and invite another question in. The instinct to keep going or to ramble comes from knowing that you haven't quite nailed it yet.

The danger is that you will keep going over the one point, and suddenly the interview is over, and you haven't said half the things you wanted to say.

Another problem that inexperienced interviewees find is that they give hostages to fortune. The presenter 'takes a flier'. That is, he asks a question from way left of field in the hope that something interesting will emerge. You start into answering the question, although you know full well that the issue is not true and has nothing to do with you.

The clock is running down, and the whole of the rest of the interview can be spent on this issue that is of no relevance whatsoever, and was not what you went there that day to talk about.

Delivering the Message

Getting the business done is a very important part of any media encounter. Every programme and publication has a particular demographic attached, a core audience or readership that you can influence, or entertain, or persuade, depending on your purpose.

You do an interview not to fill time for the radio station, or fill column inches for the newspaper company, but to speak to your audience with a particular goal in mind.

It is very frustrating to leave a studio or walk away from an interview, knowing that you didn't quite do this. That you skirted around your issues, or got sidetracked, or got taken down an unfamiliar road, and completely wasted the opportunity.

To keep yourself on track, before the interview:

- Decide the one, two or three key messages you want to get across
- Decide the stories or anecdotes you can convincingly attach to each message
- Vocalize your stories so they can be told tightly and to the point

After that try to really listen to the interviewer's question, watching out for multi-part questions.

Do your preparation well, so that you know your material, but then try to leave the notes behind. If you have notes, you will instinctively keep scanning them, missing out on what the interviewer is saying. Whereas if you trust yourself to go without the notes, you will be fully in the zone, and paying attention to what is going on.

Having the Last Word

You can improve the overall 'score' of a live interview dramatically by finishing strongly. The last few sentences or piece of interest within any exchange creates the after-view, the sense the listener has of what the whole thing has been about.

You get this opportunity by taking it.

Interviewers are always hard-pressed for time, up against a clock, hurrying interviewees because of an ad break, or a promo, or a news bulletin. But the point is, why have they invited you into studio at all if they have no time for you?

Sometimes it is a genuine pressure they are under, but other times it is a bit of an affectation, a device to keep pace in the programme.

The give-away is when the presenter says he is out of time and then proceeds to ask you three more questions.

So in the same way that you have your parachute ready to finish a live presentation, have a strong point up your sleeve ready to finish up an interview.

As the interviewer is wrapping up, ask can you make one more point, and use the opportunity to make a final punchy statement or appeal, and to leave the listener with a vital piece of information about how to contact you or find out more.

◆　　◆　　◆

Most of the examples here are framed in the scenario of a live interview for radio or television, and undoubtedly that kind of interview would be the most pressurised. But the techniques are just the same when the interview is for an online journal or for a newspaper.

You often end up doing those interviews by telephone from the comfort of your own desk or home, and it can be easy to be lulled into a false sense of security, and to make the mistake of rambling off on a tangent.

The best advice is to bear in mind all the points we have discussed here, and to keep to a few clear and well prepared messages, illustrated with strong examples.

And of course to get some good training if you are planning on starring on a primetime show any time soon!

Chapter Five

Life's A Pitch

Pitching has become something of an art form. It is that activity we have to undertake if we want to win business, make a sale, attract finance, or win support for a project. In this chapter we explore how it is done.

◆　◆　◆

FOR six years my husband and business partner Gavin Duffy was an investor on the Irish version of the *Dragons' Den* television programme. Over the years we saw all kinds of pitches – the good, the bad, and the downright barmy! Our back office had a lot of fun analysing the onscreen pitches for learning points to use in our training business.

And we have delivered pitch training programmes with Enterprise Ireland for years, putting more than 500 High Potential Start Up clients through our programmes.

During this period we received hundreds, if not thousands, of emails with 'paper pitches' from entrepreneurial hopefuls; lengthy outlines and business plans for every manner of gadget and gizmo that could attach to an ironing board.

The *Den* is a competitive process and while it is underway the investors are contracted not to accept proposals from any other source. But people have to try, and they will inevitably look around for advice or support.

Unfortunately on too many occasions the paper pitches were written so badly that the promoters were damaging their prospects rather than promoting their concept.

I don't think it is an exaggeration to say that 90 per cent of them started like this.

'My name is John and I do such and such... I attended college in... degree in biochemistry... In my career I have done all kinds of interesting things... I am passionately interested in entrepreneurship... I love the *Dragon's Den*... My product is going to change the world... I plan to take it here, there and everywhere... Can we meet for a coffee so I can tell you how you can help me?'

Or from the charity or social entrepreneurship field, they would sound like this.

'We are the society for the betterment of humankind... We were founded in... And we strive to... We have great ambitions to... We think we will change lives... We are passionately interested in humankind... We are backed by all kinds of interesting people... Can we meet so we can bore you some more?'

The first problem with both of these pitches is that when you get to paragraph four – if you stay the distance, and it is seriously doubtful that you will – you find yourself thinking, 'And the point is?' or 'What on earth has this got to do with me?'

As we have said before, we now live in a 140 character world and no one, least of all a busy investor or mentor, has the time to wade through your CV and your five year plan to find out what you want and how it is relevant to him or her. You have to frontload the relevance and the request.

The second problem in these pitches is the six 'I's in the first one and the six 'We's' in the second one. Both pitches are all about the promoter. There is absolutely nothing to attract the investor or even to encourage him or her to keep reading.

How about first telling potential investors or mentors what is in it for them? And why this idea is something they will definitely be interested in, which will fit well with their other interests and which will bring a good return?

Your personal details can be added later as background information. If the idea is a good one that instantly appeals, and it is obviously a fit, the investor may then read on down to find out about the person behind it.

So the email might go something like this instead.

'Hello Michael. I hope you don't mind a direct approach, but I want to tell you about the Wonder Widget because it fits really well with your other products and has the potential to bring you a really good return.

It is at a very interesting stage of development and you might like to hear about it before anyone else, and to consider taking some equity and entering a distribution arrangement when it goes into production later this month.

The margins are exciting and as far as we know, there are no competing products on the market, which will suit your policy of exclusivity. Here is a short outline of the development of the product and the experience of the promoters:'

This letter, as you can see, is all about Michael, the potential investor, not about the promoter. The 'ask' is very clear and upfront. It is businesslike and to the point with no faffing about.

The charitable or other type of ask needs to be equally clear, with the detail on the policies and aims of the organisation held to the end for optional reading.

'Hello Michael. The feature on you in this week's Sunday paper caught our attention. You seem to be very interested in sports education for young people and our charity is something that would certainly help you achieve your aims.

As a speaker at our event next March, you would reach your key audience and would be able to impress upon them your concerns in an area that is obviously really close to your heart.

We can't pay a speaker's fee, but would be very happy to cover your expenses on the day. And we would also like to invite you to sit on our board if that is something that would interest you.'

So again the 'ask' is clear, and the fact that it is a charity with no budget, but the plus is obvious – a focused audience and an opportunity to further a cause where there is already a well-established interest.

The aim of a paper pitch is first and foremost that it gets read. The 90 per cent I mentioned above rarely do. And you just know that the promoters are back there at the desk, fuming away at the rudeness of the recipient in not replying, when they should be blaming themselves for approaching it incorrectly in the first place.

And then of course there is the email or telephone request for the dreaded 'cup of coffee'.

Unless it is former Dragon and Insomnia Chairman Bobby Kerr you are pitching to – who presumably has a vested interest in promoting beverage drinking – forget the cup of coffee. If investors had the time to 'have a cup of coffee' with everyone who has an idea, they would be broke, and would no longer be investors.

The reason they rarely respond to the 'cup of coffee' request is that it would require leaving the office, driving to the location, having the coffee, listening to something they may have no interest in, and driving back. Thus losing the best part of a morning or an afternoon, which is probably already seriously overloaded, and which would be much better spent working on one of their existing investments.

Lots of start-ups don't seem to understand this.

They would be much better advised to write a good pitch, push the correct buttons with an investor or mentor with the correct profile, and they just might get the meeting – and the result – they want.

The Live Pitch

Once upon a time we would get a call from the CEO of a semi-state organisation. After the usual pleasantries were exchanged, he would say he needed a few people trained up. A price was agreed, a few dates put in the diary and we would turn up and deliver the training.

And then after a polite interval we'd send in an invoice and, lo and behold, a cheque would arrive in the post a few days later. It was that simple.

Nowadays, in the interest of fairness and transparency, we all have to go through public tendering with a fully scored and marked decision-making process.

This means that more and more business is won on the basis of the 'beauty parade'; the line-up of businesses who make it through the tendering process called in to a live pitch to demonstrate their credentials and competence. It can be stressful for the pitcher, but it is a great way of allowing the buyer to see how people really perform under pressure.

You can spend lots of time and money preparing the tender document, setting out your stall and proving your competence and experience. But in reality all it is doing is entering you in the competition.

It is a bit like sending in a résumé for a job. Now you have to do the interview, and excel at the interview to win the business. So here is what you need to know.

A pitch is not a test, it is a date!

You have been invited to pitch on the basis of your document, so you have obviously impressed them with your ability and your knowledge. Now they have to find out if they like you, and if they want to take this exciting new relationship to the next level.

So you need to make your pitch as lively, interesting, relevant and memorable as you know how. This is not the same thing as reading out the document they already have; or giving a slide presentation of the document they already have; or listing out facts and figures you already very carefully provided them with.

It is about:

Energy
Enthusiasm
Engagement

It is about showing them clearly that you know and love their product or service, and are ready and willing to embark on the journey of helping *them* to achieve *their* goals.

It is about:

Compliance
Competence
Connection
Completion

It is about starting a real connection where both sides feel this is good for the long haul; and where the work will be delivered to the highest possible standards over the duration of the contract.

De-formalise it

In the classic pitch, such as the one used on the *Dragons' Den*, the promoter first pitches the idea formally and uninterrupted for a number of minutes, often using visuals. This is followed by a question and answer phase, and then by a negotiation if a deal is on the table. It is very interesting to watch contrasting styles and approaches, and to see how differently people perform throughout the various phases.

There are those who stumble and stutter through the formal phase, the climb up the famous stairs making them hyper-ventilate, and the stress of television making it difficult for them to remember their own names, never mind their turnover or projected sales. But they can settle into it and some do well when the formal part is over and a real conversation around the product starts, particularly if their knowledge and passion begin to shine through.

The opposite can also happen. You see a really slick, polished initial presentation, but when the investors begin to drill down, it becomes obvious that the promoter has put all his eggs into the presentation basket and has given very little thought to the Q & A or to the negotiation.

The other kind of pitch where formality can really reduce the ability to perform is the kind used on accelerator programmes all over the world. Participants are given a slide template and told to pitch to this format on the Demo Day at the end, when investors are lined-up and the potential for big funding is at stake.

I'm not sure which genius dreamt that one up, but you may as well ask promoters to stick on a straitjacket before they start.

Recently I saw a group on an accelerator programme asked to start preparing their pitches as follows. The brackets are mine!

Slide 1: The name of the company and the promoters (That's us)

Slide 2: The problem we solve (Us again)

Slide 3: Our product or service (Yes, you guessed it, more about us!)

Slide 4: Our market (All the things we want to achieve)

Slide 5: The revenue model (The things that are going to make us money)

Slide 6: Who is behind the company (Another chance to talk about us)

Slide 7: Our competition (Those pesky people who got there before us)

Slide 8: Our Differentiator (Us again, how brilliant we are)

Slide 9: Our Request (Now we would like you to invest in us)

Slide 10: Questions (Hmmmm)

Now I happen to know, for a fact, what any self-respecting investor is thinking at this point, and it is:

I don't think so!

Ten or 15 of these dreadful pitches at one sitting and he or she is losing the plot, vowing never, ever, to come to this particular demo day again.

For a pitch to connect with an audience, whether the purpose is to make a sale or get investment, the messaging has to start with what is in it for them, not you.

The best way to do that is to leave the straitjacket at home, and to de-formalise the whole exchange, where possible, from the very start, turning it into a conversation with a purpose.

"Most of my pitches have been sales pitches and in those situations, I try to develop a personal relationship with the person opposite", says Patrick Joy, founding Director of Suretank and an Ernst and Young Entrepreneur of the Year, who says he is always looking for the opportunity to get to the heart of the issue.

"My style is to be very open, to make good eye contact, and to be very well prepared. I like to concentrate on what I consider to be the key three or four messages or points that I want to get across, and I make sure that I know my subject inside out.

"A particular pitch that stands out is the one that I gave in Norway in April 2013 to the 20 strong investment committee of the private equity company that bought two thirds of my company. I was told it was a tour de force and that my passion for the business was what got them so enthusiastic about acquiring it."

Create Rapport

So how do you create rapport? How do you walk into a room full of strangers, and come out an hour later thinking you have just met some new friends? I call it the long lost cousin effect. If you treat someone like your long lost cousin, he will begin to respond like one.

Warmth, friendliness and a genuine interest in others go a long way towards creating this impression. Familiarity does not breed contempt, as the old saying goes, it actually creates bonds and breaks down barriers. But you are making it very hard if not impossible for yourself to do warm and friendly, if you have first locked yourself into a slide deck that is all about you and your needs.

Creating rapport in a pitch is about getting a conversation going as early as you possibly can; hearing from the other side their issues, needs and concerns and responding empathetically – not heading off at a gallop into a prepared spiel which might have no relevance whatsoever to where they are at.

And the real trick is to have the confidence to do this even when they have invited you in to 'present' to them, and their people have asked your people what AV support you will need, and you arrive to see their board room all set up for a show.

And you know what you do at a show? You sit back and wait to be entertained, you don't participate.

The problem is that buying and selling is a participative process, and the result you want can't possibly happen if half the room is not participating.

People Buy People

Much in the same way as when you are presenting from a stage or a podium, if you want me to listen to you, and to believe in you, I have to be able to see you. And I don't mean that I can't see you because I got a bad seat behind the pillar. I mean I have to see *who* you are.

In a pitch you are much closer to me – right across the table or at the end of the room. It is a bit more intimate and maybe a bit more daunting for you. But I still have to be able to see you, if you want me to buy from you, or invest in you. So you have to make sure I do.

You have to use the kind of everyday language that shows your personality to best advantage, and you have to intrigue me, entertain me and educate me with examples of how you have solved similar problems to mine with previous customers or products.

Give examples and tell stories

Experienced presenters and trainers, people who are in front of rooms full of people every day, always say they prefer a whiteboard or flip-chart to slides, because the movement of walking to the whiteboard, picking up the marker, and beginning to write, takes the eyes and the ears of the room with you. They are all waiting to see what you produce.

Kieron Sparrowhawk, Chairman of MyCognition told me recently, "I love to draw an idea when pitching. A good picture is so much better to get an idea across. And then if it's strong enough, people will 'see' it, and you have them!

"They may even walk around the table and contribute to the drawing, making it 'theirs', meaning they now own part of it and you are in a collaborative process. That's awesome."

Nothing kills a presentation quicker than abstract generalisations, and dense facts and figures that we can't absorb. We crave illustrations and examples to help us understand and remember what was said.

After you leave the room, particularly if several pitches are being heard in succession, what will they remember? What will make yours standout?

The stories you tell... It's that simple.

Stories of real experiences that are relevent to this potential client will keep you in personal memory, make your communication come alive, allow your personality to show, your expertise to shine, and will allow the other side to warm to you and relate to you.

The stepping stones to success are the anecdotes and the examples. They are what win the business.

Mention the money early

Among the hundreds of people we have put through pitch training, there hasn't been one who was comfortable with the idea of bringing their fee, price or charge up early. But funnily enough, we get great reports back from those who have done it and found to their surprise and delight it works well.

Think of the traditional pitch, where you go through the slide show, and finish by asking, 'Any questions?' The first question invariably is, 'And what is all this going to cost us?' So you spend the entire Q & A phase on the back foot, justifying your price and missing out on the opportunity to be talking about benefits.

I have seen highly experienced people in a professional services firm, who charge eyewateringly large 'masters of the universe' kind of fees, give a great presentation, and then finish by sheepishly slidingly across the table a document in a folder, and mutter lamely something about the fee structure.

So the client opens the folder, starts peering into it, and again begins to query the price and the whole discussion that follows is all about that.

In a good pitch where rapport has been established early and a real conversation is taking place, you can mention your fees as boldly and as baldly as you like, and spend the rest of the encounter illustrating your experience and your commitment to the project.

If the price has been out there in the air for a while, and the conversation has moved on, the questions are more likely to be about the deliverables and there is much less onus on you to defend the number.

Believe me, this works.

And then, don't negotiate the fees until you've secured the business. Only when you have established that you are the preferred supplier should you enter any discussions about reducing the price or offering bulk discounts.

Your price is your price. It is out there, leave it there and focus on the good stuff, kicking to touch any conversation about potential wriggle room until they have said you are in line for the business.

If they can't concede that on the day, well then you can't concede anything on the price. But if they are bringing you back as the lead runner, then you can indicate there might be room for movement.

Pitching as part of a team

A team presentation has a very different dynamic to the individual pitch. It has the advantage of having colleagues along with you who will 'have your back', and mop up any questions you are not comfortable with. But it has the big disadvantage of making you all look 'clunky' and ill at ease if you haven't rehearsed well, and put together a firm strategy for how the pitch will play out on the day.

Here are a few things to remember:

Avoid 'Taxi Presentations'

The team has to look, sound and act like a team – a group of people who are aligned in message and performance, and who actually get on well with one another. The last impression you want to give is of a group who met for the first time in the taxi on the way there!

You really need to meet several times before the pitch to work out this strategy, and to do a few run-throughs. The same effort that goes into writing the proposal document should go into rehearsing for the pitch, giving particular attention to how questions will be answered.

You are not pop-up soldiers

Avoid coming across as a group of individuals, each with their own agenda, popping up in turn to say his or her piece, without any reference to what the others are saying.

You are aiming for a seamless conversation, with everyone sounding as if they are responding spontaneously to the points their own teammates are making, as well as to the questions raised from the other side.

It sounds really stilted when the team leader says: "Thank you Tara, now over to Michael to tell you about our marketing strategy".

After each team member has been invited to introduce him or herself, the team leader should put a relevant question to the first speaker from his own team. "Michael, what do you consider is really relevant for marketing here?", which sounds much more conversational. By starting each section with a question, it immediately sounds more interactive, and encourages the other side to engage throughout the pitch and to ask questions early, rather than waiting until the end.

Everyone on your team should have spoken in the first couple of minutes

It is really important that everyone hears his own voice in the room in the first few minutes, to settle down and feel 'legitimised'. Have you ever been at a meeting where the introductions were done badly, and you are left at the end of the room, unsure of when or whether you are supposed to contribute? It is soul destroying.

No team member should be sidelined in a pitch, left downstage feeling like they only have a bit part. If everyone speaks early, they are a full part of the pitch, on the balls of their feet, and ready to jump in as required.

Be ready to chip in!

The group dynamic of a team is strengthened by a conversational tone, where the participants practically finish each other's sentences and engage with the potential clients across the table. Strange as this may sound, it is what we do in normal conversation all the time.

Doing it in a pitch looks and sounds natural, and moves it away from the formal, set-piece, pop-up-soldiers, unnatural presentations we have all come to hate.

But be careful not to chip in to come to the rescue of your colleague, or to correct him. There is nothing worse than "What Sean is trying to say is....."

If one team member has spoken for several minutes uninterrupted, and is looking like running out of steam, the team leader should ask him a question to help him stay on track, or move on to the next idea by putting an appropriate question to another team member

THE Q AND A
Ask questions back

A pitch is not a one way street, and you are entitled to ask as many questions as you answer. In fact, have a few good questions ready for the Q and A segment, especially in pitches where, despite your best efforts, you have been locked into a formal first half. If you have succeeded in deformalising the whole process, you will have been asking questions throughout, and making the whole event interactive.

Get clarification before answering

When the client asks a question, clarify the information they are looking for by saying something like 'Am I right in thinking you would like to know more about how we propose to deal with security? Great, I'll give you our views on that now, and then I'll ask John to give you a few examples of where it has worked well.'

In doing this you have achieved a few things. You have just 'checked in' with the client, you have made sure your information is correctly targeted, and you have also given your colleague notice to come on in with some examples when you are finished.

Find the concern before giving the answer

If the client asks – Will this work be carried out by you or other colleagues? – where is the concern, do you think?

It may be that they believe a second division team will actually be put to work on the contract, after the A team has been drafted in just to make the pitch. Or it may be that they think your company is really too busy to give this project the attention it deserves. Or they are concerned about the depth of your organisation.

Don't rattle off an answer before first finding out what is their specific concern and then answer appropriately.

AID

Remember Address, Illustrate and Direct from the presentations chapter? Use the technique here as well to take control of the questioning, and steer it towards your strong messages. Every question then becomes a great opportunity to highlight your strengths.

If you don't know, say so

Never spoof the answer to a question. If addressing the issue isn't going to work, and you just don't have the facts to hand, say so.

Not knowing the answer can be turned into a positive. It is a great excuse to get back later with the information that was looked for, which is an opportunity to strengthen the relationship, to thank them again for having you in to pitch, and possibly to get some immediate feedback on how it went.

Ending the Q and A

You can't ask too many questions but sometimes you can be met with silence if you finish the presentation with "Thank you for listening, have you any questions?"

It is often better for the team leader to say "We are coming to the end of our presentation, but before we wrap up we want to make sure we have addressed all the issues. (Address one of the clients specifically, by name). John/Mary have we answered all your concerns about the time frame or is there anything else we can cover now for you in the time we have left?"

If there are still no questions, the team leader can use this opportunity to restate the key differentiators of his team.

♦   ♦   ♦

All the points above have been developed through working with hundreds of companies and individuals over the years on pitch training, and then getting feedback afterwards; hearing great stories of deals won, contracts signed and investment achieved.

But it is only theory until you put it into practice. So you need to rehearse yourself and your team prior to a big pitch until you are so comfortable with the material that you can focus your full attention on the other side – and work out what is really going on in the room at all times, so you can adapt accordingly.

The On-the-Spot or Elevator Pitch

New politicians often talk about having the notes for their 'stump' speech in the pocket or handbag at all times. This is the multi-purpose, fits-all-occasions speech that can be whipped out at a moments notice when called upon to say a few words, topped and tailed to suit the particular event.

The 'after' impression they are aiming for is of someone on top of their game, in control, with a grasp of the facts, and ready and willing to deliver results. Whether they achieve that or not is, of course, another story.

For the rest of us, the elevator pitch is similar – a form of words that describes our current project to best advantage, which can be called into good effect should we meet someone influential by chance, well – in the elevator.

The idea is to get vital information out quickly, efficiently and with enough style to impress, and enough of a hook to leave them wanting to know more – all delivered in the time it takes to move between floors.

Anyone running a business, or developing a product or service, needs an elevator pitch for a chance meeting with a financier, a potential backer or an industry expert who might open a few doors.

It is also really useful at the networking events we all seem to attend lately, for telling people what you do, or what problem you solve, quickly and clearly and without boring the pants off them!

'I make these really cool office chairs that look great and will allow you to sit in a better position, reducing back pain. If I was to drop one around to your office this week for you to try out, what colour would you go for?'

In the corporate world, the elevator pitch is a handy tool for reputation enhancement and career advancement. Made to look natural and spontaneous, it is the difference between an awkward silence on the walk from the car park to the front door with senior management, and an opportunity to shine.

'You might like an update on the Benson project, Jennifer? Sales are good and we are delighted with the three new client signings. Actually, now that I think of it, the team would really love your view on the revised marketing strategy. Would you have time to drop down to us later today?'

That sounds smart, focused and interested, and definitely beats mumbling about the weather, or peering at the mobile phone for cover.

Whatever the circumstances, the elevator pitch needs to do a few things. It needs to give a snapshot of the current situation, a sense of progression, and an idea of how things can be in the future. And above all, it needs to be fair and accurate, and not an exaggeration, or it will backfire.

And if you are at that networking event, watch out for a faraway look coming into the eyes of the person you are speaking with. That is your signal to change the subject. They are clearly not interested in your beautiful ergonomic chairs, so connect on a personal level instead, and talk about the football.

Chapter Six

Meetings That Make Sense

In this chapter, you will hear about the things that make meetings work, and also about the things that make them falter, fizzle out and completely waste everyone's time! And there is also a full run down on how to become a really efficient and high performing Chairperson.

♦   ♦   ♦

HE is one of the most affable people I know, the kind of guy lots of people want to be. He is a very good looking 55 and keeps himself really trim and fit. He runs a great business, has a beautiful home, an amazing wife and family and drives a fast car.

Out socialising, he is the life and soul of the party. You could bring him anywhere, and as a friend, he's the very best.

The problem is that I can't stand to be in a meeting that he chairs, and neither can most of the other people around the table.

We had occasion some years back to serve on the same board, where he had been elected Chair, and I began to dread the meetings, knowing that they would be a nightmare of late starts, indecision, rambling thoughts, long-winded statements, and absolutely no direction given to anyone or anything.

As the board got into the swing of its lifespan, I took him aside and gently pointed out that people had lives and homes to go to, and that really we should try to keep the meetings to an hour in length, or an hour and a half at a push. The previous month, the meeting had run for three hours, and by the end of it people were seriously disgruntled.

He heard me out with grace and acceptance of well-intentioned feedback, and then proceeded to let the meeting run for three hours all over again. This time the participants were fulminating as they left for home, and threatening all kinds of dire consequences on his head, which he was and remains to this day blissfully unaware of.

Because he mistakenly thinks that he is doing a great job; that the lovely affable personality he is blessed with, and which is great on the social scene, works just as well in the boardroom.

- He thinks that starting a meeting at 10.20 as opposed to 10am is just giving people space to hang up their coats, get their coffee and socialise for a bit.
- He thinks that chatting away until 10.40 is opening the meeting in a relaxed way, with plenty of time to reflect on last month's activities.
- He thinks that allowing people to ramble on without summarising, or noting action points, is giving them space to express themselves.
- He thinks that asking every person there to re-cap on all they have been doing, whether they have anything to say or not, is fair and equitable, when he should be seeing that pertinent issues drive the agenda.
- He thinks that the clock is a decoration on the wall.

As you sit there, with the time going on and a thousand things to be done back at the desk or at home, and you have to listen to someone make up a report which is no different to the one they gave last month, you start planning your resignation from the board.

As a performing leader, a Chair's first responsibility is to use the meeting as a touchpoint to keep the team focused, aligned, moving forward and above all believing in the project and the potential outcomes. A poorly run meeting will put everyone in a bad mood, and halve productivity for the rest of the day.

As an attendee at a meeting you have different responsibilities – to prepare well, to report clearly, to make evidence-based contributions, and to hear what others are saying, and we'll come to that shortly.

But let's look at Chairing first, an opportunity to really perform as a leader, or to crash and burn, like my friend above.

Chairing a Meeting

There are four 'must haves' for a well-run meeting:

- Time Constraints
- Good Preparation
- Solid Presentations
- A Chair who is in control

Time Constraints

We are all busy with a hundred things to fit into our day, so we want to know when the meeting is going to start, and equally when it is going to end. So it is important to state clearly on the agenda the start and finish times. How many meeting notifications have you received with a start time, and nothing at all about how long each item is going to take, or when you might get out of there?

Some people schedule meetings at offbeat times to make the start time more memorable, and to avoid people allowing themselves a few minutes grace. So if you say the meeting is at 2pm, they will straggle in at 2.05 or 2.10, whereas if you call the meeting for 2.10 in the first place, they are likely to be there on time.

Worth a try, but I'd be inclined to call the meeting for 1.45 arrival and coffee, saying it will kick off at 2pm sharp. But then you have to follow through and start at 2pm on the button, so that those who are late miss the top of the meeting and make a better effort to be there next time.

No point in rewarding the latecomers by waiting for them, and punishing those on time by leaving them sitting around!

Another good idea is to have the time you are allocating for each item on the agenda clearly stated; ten minutes for item four, fifteen minutes for item seven and so on. Deadlines make people reach decisions, and a strong Chair with an eye on the clock reminds people that the time for that particular item is coming to a close. So people make their minds up, and the meeting is more productive.

Preparation

As the Chair, you need to prepare well for the meeting. Draw up your agenda, with the timings attached, and circulate it a number of days beforehand. Seems obvious, but it is amazing how few Chairs actually do it.

The agenda should include the specific issues and the clear-cut objectives to be addressed, with a note attached to each agenda item on what the aim is – a discussion, an information piece, a decision, or a recommendation to the executive. The board works much better if they know exactly what is expected of them.

If you want any of the attendees to deliver a presentation, or to provide a written response for the meeting, state clearly what duration or length is required and what format the input is to take.

Presentations or Reports

It is up to the Chair to see that contributing participants plan their piece well, and understand to deliver it in a clear and interesting manner within the prescribed time. Ideally you should contact them in advance, to firstly ask them to make the contribution, but then to brief them on exactly what you want from the item.

So you might say:

"We don't like being talked at, and we are quite informal, so no need for power point, or to feel you have to pump the facts at us. We would much prefer a conversation around the issue, and to hear your insights, with the facts and figures on a sheet that we can look at afterwards. How does that sound?"

or

"I'd like a short presentation from you – no longer than 5 minutes – giving an overview of the situation, but then you need to be prepared to take questions for 15 or 20 minutes. They are a very interactive board and will want to get to the heart of how this came about. But don't worry, they are looking forward to meeting you, and know that what you have to say will be really interesting and relevant."

So you are doing two things here as Chair – you are setting up the presenter to contribute well, and you are 'producing' your meeting, making sure that things will be relevant and interesting for everyone there.

A Chair who is in control

A good Chair is clearly on top of the material, has briefed people well, has an obvious plan, communicates it well to all present and runs the meeting efficiently and well.

Tom Savage was my Chairman on the Board of RTÉ, the Irish National Broadcaster, where I served for five years and I personally really enjoyed his style. He had a talent for making each person in the room feel that the words they had just uttered were the most important thing that had been said that day. But then to move rapidly on to the next item, before you lost the run of yourself entirely!

As a State board, there was also the luxury of a very strong secretariat, so the board pack and agenda arrived like clockwork three or four days before the monthly meeting, allowing you plenty of time to do your reading and prepare for the meeting.

But if I was to pick out the key things that I have noted good Chairs do, over many years of observing them – and trying to be one myself – it is that:

- They open the meeting very pointedly at the specific time, welcoming the participants and thanking them for their attendance. And they remind participants the time at which the meeting will be concluding.
- They state the goals and specific objectives of the meeting; what's for discussion, what is to be decided, and what is to be actioned.
- At the start of each agenda item, they make a 30-60 second opening statement on the item and solicit quick views from around the room, before the item is discussed in depth.
- They never go around the room in order of seating, saying: "We'll start with you Pat and go round this way and hear everyone's views." They know that it is better to hop around, keeping everyone awake and on their toes.
- They never allow two people to talk at once, or

for side-bar conversations to emerge, and they never discuss anything but the item at this point on the agenda.

- They announce the speaker they are going to come to after the next speaker, to allow that person set themselves up. For example, "I'll come to Claire after Hilary. Hilary do you agree with what Colm said?"

- They make it clear that they are winding up the discussion on this item very shortly, and they keep mentioning the magic word "decision". For example, "Ok, have we any final views before we make our decision, and go on to the report from the Sales Division?"

- They feel consensus emerging, and move quickly for a decision. They say things like: "Ok, I am keen to move on because I want to allow ample time to hear the updates from Colin about the project and we also have to hear from Jacinta about the exhibition".

- They compliment those who make concise contributions, rather than criticising those who talk too much. They know that positive reinforcement gets results.

- They sit back and allow those who wish to express an opinion do so, before coming in with one of their own. They know not to enter into dialogue, as this can dilute the authority of their chairmanship.

- They take notes, specifically when decisions have been reached, drawing attention to the fact that the decision has been taken and noted, and the item closed.

- They only call for a vote as a last resort. They know that it can be divisive, and use it sparingly as a means of wrapping something up.
- They never let a meeting fizzle out at the end or splutter to a close. With 10 minutes to go, they remind everyone that they plan on finishing at the agreed time, as per the agenda, and they call for a wrap-up on the last item and any other business.
- They make a one-minute closing statement including a brief reminder of decisions taken, a mention of important follow-up actions to be undertaken, including deadlines, and they thank participants and end the meeting formally and authoritatively.

If you can remember to do most of these things stylishly and well at important meetings you chair, add in some humour and a genuine interest in people, you will be a good leader and teams will enjoy your meetings.

Is This Meeting Really Necessary?

Did you spot the key words in the last paragraph? They were 'important meetings'. I am hugely mindful of the fact that years worth of human lives are being wasted, right at this very moment, in offices and concerns all over the world at lengthy, pointless and meaningless meetings.

There are meetings to set up meetings and meetings to discuss previous meetings and meetings to discuss future meetings. And people 'sitting in' on meetings and 'observing' meetings and referencing meetings, and minuting meetings.

And you would sometimes wonder what it is all for, or what is the real objective with any of them?

But sometimes having the luxury of an overarching ethos makes the goal for all human transactions much clearer.

Leonard Moloney, SJ, was the principal of Clongowes Wood and Belvedere Colleges for over ten years each, and gave chunks of his life to meetings in each role. I once heard him described by former Taoiseach John Bruton as 'an extraordinary leader'.

He told me a story recently about trying to use every opportunity to communicate to the pupils, or the staff members, or the board, or the parents – regardless of the content or the purpose of the actual meeting – the idea that there are always options if we know how to see them.

"I had such a long day, we had a meeting of the trustees, and then some staffing issues, and the board of management and then with the new principal, and I sat down and happened to watch this movie, Evan Almighty. In it Morgan Freeman played God. Morgan is talking to this guy, this Congressman, and he says, when people ask me for the gift of patience, do you think I should give them the gift of patience, or the opportunity to be patient?

"And it was just a brilliant little vignette – God offering real respect for human freedom and all the time offering possibilities. So in my style of meeting, that's what I would want to be doing."

This is a great example of someone knowing their purpose. But the need to get a serious piece of business over the line is also a strong driver for a focused meeting.

Former Tánaiste and leader of the Progressive Democrats Mary Harney finds that preparing really well and communicating the issues clearly in advance is crucial. She described the cabinet meeting, at which the Irish cancer service reform was agreed, as one of the most meaningful of her career, as she got a really significant decision through.

"The number of hospitals providing cancer surgery would be reduced from 31 to 8 specialist centres with multidisciplinary teams. Ireland is now achieving substantially better outcomes for cancer patients."

But for the rest of us, meetings can often be tedious, unfocused gatherings of colleagues or volunteers who haven't prepared properly, and who are inclined to speak around in circles unless, of course, you take the approach of entrepreneur and strategy trainer Elliot Jacobs.

"I really like the daily huddle – the meeting that takes place standing up, with clear goals around communicating immediate issues and getting quick decisions. No one takes too long to get to the point, and it is over in a few minutes. It's very effective."

So before you rush to call a meeting, or several meetings, to try out the chairmanship skills we have been discussing, you have to ask yourself a few questions:

- Is a meeting at this point the only way to fulfil my objectives?
- Is a meeting the BEST way to fulfil my objectives?
- What are the alternatives?
- Will a meeting use my time and my colleagues' time to our best advantage?
- Is this meeting only being held because it's Friday and that's what we do on Fridays?
- Could an email, with several key questions, get a quicker and clearer result?
- Could a conference call get the same result?

If you decide that face time and a full meeting is absolutely essential to move the project along, you now have to decide who needs to be at the meeting. The fewer the better is probably a good rule of thumb – the duration of the meeting directly proportionate to the number of people attending.

But you do have to consider:

- Who are you obliged to invite?
- Who can cause trouble if not invited?
- Who can give you what you want?
- Who is in favour of your objective?
- Who will oppose your objective?
- Who is on the fence?

So now send out a memo of invitation. If you are absolutely sure that this meeting needs to take place, then take it seriously and structure it to get the results you want.

The memo gets the meeting into peoples diaries and confirmed well before time. It makes people realise that they have to show up and bring something to the picnic. And it is a good way of performing like a leader, even where you are not an official Chair and cannot assume that title.

The alternative – "Why don't you and the team drop into my office at 4pm" – is more casual, and people will take that meeting as relaxed and not requiring any special preparation.

Understanding the Meeting Dynamic

No matter where they take place, or in what language they are conducted, all meetings follow a particular pattern.

Someone states a case.
Others support or knock that case.
Others propose an alternative case or cases.
Alliances are formed.
Movement occurs.
A decision is made and minuted.

To get your proposals over the line you need to understand

the meeting dynamic and the value of timing; you have to spot movement, and you may well need to have acquired some allies before the day.

If you have one or two people teed up to support your proposal before it has ever come up, you are half-way there.

It is said that most board decisions are actually made in the corridor outside the boardroom, or on the golf course the day before. I don't play golf, so I can't confirm that one, but I can appreciate where the phrase 'corridors of power' originates. I do know that strategic alliances are formed well in advance of a big meeting, and the decisions in the room are often a foregone conclusion.

Let's just call it office politics – not a dirty word, as some people think, but simply an understanding of the sources and uses of power.

When we are working with groups on meeting skills we do an exercise that really demonstrates how this works. I have seen senior partners in law and accountancy firms enter the role play with gusto, and really enjoy the results.

We give the group a topic to discuss, something out of the normal course of business so they can really let their hair down. The topic might be, for example, that we are redecorating this board room; what style should we go for and how much should we spend on it. Then we give 'stances' to the participants, which their colleagues are not party to. So Dearbhla is hell-bent on a blue boardroom, John wants yellow, Peter doesn't give a toss what colour it is as long as John doesn't get his own way, Grainne wants to spend nothing, thinks it is fine as it is, and so on.

The exercise is to see who gets their own way, and the funny part, for us as trainers, is that we can always predict with a complete certainty who that will be! Because all meetings follow a pattern, and once you know the pattern, you are far more likely to achieve your goal.

Gavin Duffy, TV *Dragon* investor and veteran of a number of boards, has worked out a way of spotting alliances in a meeting, which you may not have been privy to beforehand, and responding with a strategy of your own.

He calls it the:

Shut up
Sit up
Tot up
Put up
Mop up

method of working a meeting to your advantage.

Shut Up is first and it is surprising to many to learn that those who talk the least, particularly at the start of a meeting, can influence the most. Too often we land into a meeting bursting with the brilliance of our great information and dying to throw it all on the table.

But this is when resistance is at its highest and the best of ideas can get lost because positions are adopted before people fully understand the concepts, positions they can't go back on later without losing face.

Often it is not what you say or how much you say that carries the day in a crucial meeting. It is all about when you make your case. People who stay quiet and listen can work out exactly where others are coming from and get their timing right.

Sit Up comes next. This is where you pay close attention to what is being said, asking questions for clarity, and noting from the body language, exchanged glances, and other non verbal signals who is aligned with whom.

Tot Up is where you start to see who is for and against the proposal on the table, and who may be aligned with yours when you land it. There will be those at the table who are against the current proposal, because they are against the person who made it, and who will gladly support an alternative. Any alternative. Particularly when things have been going around for a while and fresh thinking is clearly needed.

Put Up You feel the movement, and you put your proposal up on the table fast. Your timing is right, people will go for it, and you can start to bring it home.

Mop Up "Well it seems we have some consensus there so will we take that as a decision? Great, we can move on then to the finance report." And guess what? You are home and hosed. Your proposal has just been carried.

To sum up, all meetings have three phases, or three phases for each agenda item.

> **The Presentation phase** – When participants set out their stalls
>
> **The Positioning phase** – When participants check out the lie of the land
>
> **The Movement phase** – When consensus begins to emerge.

The challenge is in staying on your toes while the first two phases are underway, so that you are fully alert to when the movement phase starts, and poised to seize the moment.

But don't let it drag on. As soon as you have the bones of an agreement grab it, verbalise it, note it and confirm it back to the meeting straight away.

Participating rather than Chairing or Organising

As an active participant in a meeting, you will have to prepare properly if you want your contribution to mean anything and to resonate. It's true you won't have the same onus to keep the show on the road as the Chair or Organiser, but you have a personal responsibility not to waffle either.

You will know from attending unproductive meetings that the ones that go pear-shaped usually have:

- No specific objectives for the meeting, its leader or its participants.
- No agenda set or circulated in advance.
- Too many participants or the wrong participants.
- Unprepared participants
- Participants with no understanding of the politics
- Contributors who talk too much.
- Contributors who inflict Death by PowerPoint on their colleagues
- Too many digressions and interruptions.
- Time wasted on "Why" rather than "How".
- Mixed final decisions due to lack of closure and weak chairing

We can blame poor chairmanship for lots of this but we can also blame poor participation. To become an effective contributor to meaningful meetings, you should make a decision, right now, that you will never 'sit in' on a meeting again.

Your time is far too valuable.

You will only attend a meeting with a very specific objective in mind – to hear something, to learn something, to contribute something or to influence an outcome.

You are not a spectator and you have to know why you are there and what you hope to get out of the experience.

Ask yourself –

- Why am I attending this meeting?
- Why am I going to contribute to this meeting?
- What do I want to achieve at the meeting?
- What do I want to achieve following the meeting?

If you have been asked to contribute background information for an agenda item, particularly when reporting up to the board, prepare your report to the time slot allowed, keeping it simple and interesting.

Non-executive directors come from a wide variety of backgrounds, and while they may be very experienced in corporate governance they may actually know little about the technical side of the business.

Don't blind them with science or use industry jargon which they won't embarrass themselves by asking you to explain. Keep your presentation in simple language, and use plenty of examples to illustrate what you are saying.

And front load your information! Don't keep the good stuff till last and don't make the board work to find out what you are on about. You are supposed to cut through all the detail, and bring clarity and insight. That is why you are there.

One time on the RTÉ board we got a complex report from a senior member of the team with an executive summary that had about three lines, more or less saying – you asked for this report, here it is, there are loads of findings in there, go and root for them yourself.

The report was lengthy and part of a huge board pack that had come out that month. As I was settling down on the sofa with a heavy sigh to tackle into it, my daughter said to me 'You are going to need chocolate with that one, Mam'.

She was right!

♦   ♦   ♦

Meetings are a necessary evil for most of us, taking up far more of our time than we perhaps like. But with some thought and preparation, they can be interesting, productive, and even enjoyable.

And don't forget they are a brilliant touchpoint for catching up with colleagues, and for having those side-bar conversations – both personal and business – that can lead on to so much.

As a lively, engaged and well prepared Chair or contributor, you can make the whole experience better for yourself and your colleagues, and get the results you want efficiently and quickly.

Good customer engagement can solve a bigger problem than the one on the table

Michael O'Leary is the CEO of HRM, and described this meeting where listening, and reacting correctly, turned things for his client organisation.

"We have a consulting arm to our business HRM Consult, which supports organisations in addressing a range of talent related challenges. On a recent occasion, a high-growth technology customer shared concerns about the need to retain two senior technologists who were central to a very significant US customer bid, one that could really change the fortunes of the organisation.

"The CEO was bothered about their engagement levels and he felt rumbles of discontent. He wanted to know how much he would have to pay them to ultimately ensure they didn't leave. But rather than offer silly money, which only creates a bigger problem elsewhere, we asked to do an engagement audit across the organisation.

"We found that he was right. The two engineers were planning an exit but their discontent was not about money – they were happy with their compensation. It was about the fact that they had to initially fund their own expenses, travel, accommodation etc., which were considerable and they often had to wait too long to have them reimbursed.

They had raised the matter on previous occasions but nothing had been done.

"At one level they were racking up and bearing interest costs but when the issue was left unaddressed, it festered and ultimately they did not like what this said about the organisation or how it treated employees. It was a small issue which had been let get out of hand and was about to break the back of the organisations opportunity."

Chapter Seven

Negotiating

In this chapter we look at closing the odds when it comes to achieving our goals in a negotiation, something I heard defined beautifully by a colleague recently as 'the art of achieving wise outcomes'.

◆   ◆   ◆

GOING into a tense negotiation is the modern day version of going into battle.

We arm ourselves with all the facts and figures, sharpen the saw with strong self-talk, gather up the team and motivate them well, choose the location for the bout, apply the war-paint, and head on over the hill hoping we are smarter, or faster or more agile than the other side.

But of course it isn't a battle, and there shouldn't be winners or losers. The strongest negotiations are based on a collaborative model – an understanding from both sides that the goal is solving a shared problem, and reaching that outcome in a dignified and respectful way.

On a breakfast TV panel recently, we were discussing the proposed purchase of the Irish government's shareholding in Aer

Lingus by AIG, and I made the point that the staff were central to the negotiations; that without their buy-in, any change in control would be slower and more cumbersome.

Another panellist, a newspaper journalist, asked me where I got my quaint notions from. He said the staff were totally unimportant to the negotiations, the only thing that mattered was the politics involved.

And that is exactly where negotiations crash and burn.

Just as well the gentleman in question is a good journalist, because he will never be a manager, or a negotiator. If those on either side of a divide actually feel that the people in an organisation are unimportant, and let those feelings be known, the thing is doomed before it even starts.

Negotiations are conducted by people, about people, for an outcome that is going to affect people. Yes, things like the politics, and the stocks and shares, and who is ultimately going to pay the bill, are hugely relevant and important.

But on the day, around the table, it is people who will do the talking, and ultimately find resolution or not, depending on their own attitude and preparedness.

Denis O'Brien has been heard to jocosely ask guests in his reception area "Are you buying, or are you selling?", and it is a fundamental question. But you don't often have the luxury of that kind of clarity at the outset.

If you want to become a good negotiator, a good place to start is probably with the realisation that you have been negotiating successfully every day, all your life, and others have been negotiating equally successfully with you.

You negotiated a loan to buy your house; with your neighbour to stop parking his car in front of your gate; with your partner to go away for the weekend with the team; with your best friend to return – eventually – the box set of *Breaking Bad*.

Your kids have been negotiating successfully with you, since forever, for extra time on the X-box, more pocket money, an extra hour out playing on a bright night, a later curfew during half-term and so on. And they are darn good at it.

They marshal the facts, present them well, add in a bit of emotional blackmail, give you those eyes, the killer smile, and the job is done.

So negotiating is an activity we are well practised at, and one that is relatively simple when the stakes are low and the outcome is not earth shattering. It gets tougher when the bar is higher and the outcome is going to seriously affect you or those you are responsible for.

Failed negotiations can lead to loss of money or jobs, businesses closing, relationships breaking down, de-motivated teams and lots of other disastrous consequences.

I believe that a successful negotiation has to start with respect for the other side and with a genuine desire to play the ball and not the man. The other side is not an enemy, an opponent or an adversary. You are not heading into a rout at the crossroads, hurls aloft; or a game of rugby where the heaviest pack will gain the inches. It is not about bulldozing, besting or bullying people.

It is about doing the homework, being very clear on needs, presenting the strongest case you can, listening well, understanding your BATNA and, as the song goes, knowing when to hold and knowing when to fold.

As the founding fathers of modern negotiation, Roger Fisher and William Ury put it:

"The reason you negotiate is to produce something better than the results you can obtain without negotiating. What are those results? What is that alternative? What is your BATNA – your Best Alternative To a Negotiated Agreement? That is the standard against which any proposed agreement should be measured."

Start with the Homework

Good research is key to the success of any negotiation, something that is easier than ever to accomplish. So there is no excuse. You can find out lots about the other side on websites, social and traditional media, and through having discussions with key people – remembering through which particular prism the view is coming.

- The company website and their published material = their view
- Newspaper and online coverage = a moderated (journalist's) view
- What is said on social media = external (perhaps uninformed) view
- Former employees = external (perhaps disgruntled) view
- Strategic partner = internal (probably informed) view
- Site or plant visit = bird's eye view
- Current employees = internal (ground up) view
- Current management = internal (top down) view

This kind of research will yield some really good perspective on the other side and hopefully on the team they will be fielding on the day. Knowing and understanding past form of the players is very helpful, and any insight to their background, experience and drivers will inform how you approach the meeting.

A reach out before the event is always good – some personal contact that begins to establish rapport and a degree of trust – also some agreement on the agenda, if possible, and ground rules.

Social media is one way to reach out informally. Favouriting and sharing other people's posts is a great way of showing you care. We are all flattered by it.

But it's not enough on its own. It should be followed by a formal email or a good old fashioned telephone conversation to break the ice and reinforce the notion that the problem will be put on the table, and discussed dispassionately, with the objective of finding a workable resolution for all.

Unplanned negotiations take a different kind of preparation, more of a mental preparedness, and an agility that allows you see all the options and go down all the avenues.

Scott McDonald is the CEO of Noise Solutions Inc, based in Alberta, Canada. In 2009, when the world economy went pear-shaped, he had to hold his nerve in the face of illness and the banks playing hardball. He told me he had to respond really quickly to negotiate the terms with stakeholders that would allow his business to survive.

"We had expanded our company to include US sales teams – our first real boots on the ground in the US – and sales were expanding like crazy. Our revenue in the US went from 10 per cent to 55 per cent of our global sales. We looked like superstars.

"Then the world economy collapsed, and our sales simply dried up, and the US fell to between 2–3 per cent of our revenues. Oh, and this all happened while I was in bed for 12 days with the H1N1 virus and unaware of the situation.

"When I awoke, I found my company in crisis, my business partner checked out of the business and staff wondering what the hell was going to happen.

Then my bank called a $2.5 million loan due in 30 days.

"I negotiated a 90-day extension on the loan – why do banks always charge you more money when you have none? – worked on refinancing all of my plant property and equipment, hired a CFO, and negotiated quicker pay terms from my existing clients. One client found out about our situation and paid out $1.5 million in less than 24 hours.

"We had to downsize the company and temporarily reduce staff and salaries by over 60 per cent, through wage reduction and layoffs, 120 staff to 40. This bought us the time needed to wait through the economic blip and enter the new world economy. I have never had a demand loan since."

Through reacting quickly, negotiating well and listening to the ideas from his core team, Scott turned his business around and within a few years had built it right back up.

Choosing the team

We all have characteristic communication styles under pressure and an awareness of these is crucial before going into a negotiation. The people you need to strenuously avoid bringing onto your negotiating team are:

The Commander

This one is the Boss, and has the sign on the door to prove it. Very often an alpha personality, he may have spent too much time in dressing-rooms listening to pep talks along the lines of 'make every blow a wound'.

Mistakenly, he thinks that the game is about letting the other side know, at every opportunity, that they are losing. He plays 'dirty' before, during and after the negotiation.

He doesn't give the other side a chance to prepare properly, and during the meeting may use threatening language, make personal remarks, demand impossible concessions, or use every available opportunity to upset the other side.

The Commander thinks that this is being powerful; a 'don't mess with me' kind of negotiator.

The Contrarian

This one has a fixed position, at extreme odds with the other side, and thinks that holding the line at all costs is what it is about. She takes no responsibility for the outcome, finding satisfaction in withstanding each and every perceived attack on her stance.

There is only one result, as far as she is concerned, the complete and total about face of the opposition, and the acknowledgement that she was right all along.

The Calamatist

This one sees danger and adversity everywhere. There be monsters out there. His nervousness and unease as he steps through the door for the negotiation is palpable and noted by everyone in the room. It doesn't matter what words he uses now, his body language has already said it all.

As the meeting progresses, he may overreact to what is said, he may blurt out assertions rather than cite facts, he may become emotive. He may not have his brain in gear.

The Circumventor

This one is a straw in the wind, and is so anxious for a resolution, any resolution, that she comes across as weak and indecisive.

She doesn't have a BATNA, makes concessions too easily, tries one thing and then another, and is absolutely terrified of deadlock.

She too takes no responsibility for the outcome, and afterwards will blame all kinds of external circumstances for the lack of a result.

The Player

The wing men and women you need with you on the day of a crucial negotiation know all those characters above, and know to never show up that way themselves!

Good team members are:

- Willing to do good research
- Resilient and focused

- Capable of listening as much as talking
- Flexible and willing to compromise

And they know to:

- Leave personal feelings outside the door
- Leave judgemental and critical language outside the door
- Manage their non verbal signals
- Communicate clearly and directly

Those are the team members who will have your back, who will be mindful and present, and who will be a real asset on the day.

Planning the Strategy

Earlier I quoted Roger Fisher and William Ury. Their seminal book *Getting to Yes* has been on the business best-seller list for years. Their central premise is that you always had to leave something for the other side; if you allow everyone gain some small thing, a negotiation has every chance of concluding satisfactorily.

In series three of *House of Cards*, US President Frank Underwood and Russian President Petrov are in the Kremlin negotiating late into the night on a wide ranging deal covering US involvement in the Middle East. In the earlier away game, from the Russian perspective, Petrov had been firmly in Commander mode, as described earlier, but now on the home leg, he has softened somewhat and seems more open to movement.

Underwood, spotting his opportunity, moves into classic 'Getting to Yes' territory, and says: 'Why don't we start mapping out what a potential agreement might look like?"

So in this example they haven't reached agreement yet; they are not even close, but just for the exercise, a good negotiator is suggesting that they park the objections for the moment and start talking about what possible common ground might look like.

By doing this, each side inevitably start being more favourably disposed towards each other, and starts using the language of agreement, which might even lead to real agreement. It is spotting the opportunity, and moving in. Nice one Frank!

Your strategy planning session should start with your BATNA – the Best Alternative to a Negotiated Agreement – which ultimately protects you from accepting terms that are too unfavourable to you, and from rejecting terms that might be in your interest to accept. Having a good understanding of this hugely increases your negotiating power.

You work out your BATNA based on defining:

- Issues and problems – not people or emotions
- Interests and genuine needs – not positions or stances

And then you get really creative, and start working on places where you can find, suggest, or invent mutual gain.

And you use evidence, facts and history to platform these places, not generalisations, or feelings, or bias.

Your strategy also needs to take into account a whole bunch of what ifs:

- What if the proposed agreement is better than our BATNA? – Accept it
- What if the proposal is worse than our BATNA? – Keep negotiating
- What if they will not move? – Start listing options for mutual gain
- What if there is absolute deadlock? – Can each side attain small goals in a distributive way?
- What if you are coming to the end of the line? – Take a break and try again

Walking the Walk

Success in negotiation is very much about anticipation – working out what the other side might do, how they might behave on the day, and preparing accordingly.

Here are some of the situations you might encounter:

Difficult or intransigent people: These need to be spotted early and disarmed, usually by giving their inputs plenty of attention, and reflecting back to them what they are saying, so that they know you are listening. A good opening phrase is "I hear you say....".

"John, I hear you say that you have serious concerns about the Cork operation, and that you have regard for the long serving staff there. I think we share those concerns. I would like to suggest......" and go on to make your point.

Another good move is to clarify the concern before answering a question. So John asks a straight question: "What are you suggesting we do about the Cork operation?"

You reply: "Sure, happy to discuss Cork next, but can I ask you John, for clarity, where are your specific concerns in that regard?"

The chances are, he will explain his concerns – the staff, or the costs, or the media response, or whatever it might be. And then your answer becomes much more focused.

We all love to explain things. We all love being put into the position of 'expert'. We enjoy being asked for advice, and being given the floor to expand. It is very hard to fight when you are listened to attentively, and those around you are sitting up, paying attention, nodding, obviously very interested. It is seriously disarming.

Hidden agendas: Asking for clarity is your main tool here. The best negotiators listen twice as much as they talk, and the listening follows carefully posed questions, phrased softly.

"Just so I am absolutely clear here, would you mind explaining the background to that?"

"I know you have probably been over this many times, but for the benefit of my team here, could you give us a synopsis of the situation to date?"

"Am I right in thinking that this point is very central for you? Could you explain why?"

"You have mentioned several concerns. Could I ask you to prioritize those concerns in order of importance to you?"

Aggression: It takes two to start a fight and there will never be a row if you do not rise to the bait, regardless of what is said. You have to think of pantomime players going 'oh yes you did', 'oh no you didn't', 'oh yes you did', 'oh no you didn't'; the pitch and tone getting higher and louder, the pace getting faster and faster.

This is a negotiation falling apart.

"Yes, but…" is a much better response than a flat "No", which begs for immediate counter disagreement. Even when you disagree vehemently with the other side, it is better not to say so baldly, as it brings the language of disagreement centre stage.

You should instead be working to allow the language of agreement to flourish. So instead of risking starting a row, you say: "I completely understand why you hold that view, but I'd like to explain my point of view."

Or you could say: "That's one way of looking at it, certainly, but could we now take a few minutes to look at it this way?"

The language in these examples is gentle, even conciliatory, but don't ever confuse that with weakness. It is actually a strength.

Deadlock: Giving away minor points in the hope of making a major one can be effective, conceding things that you have found out – by listening – are important to the other side, but not so huge to you. Movement is infectious. Give a little and they will too.

But know that movement is only spotted by those who are open to it. People who are locked into remembering a rehearsed position are using up all their brain's RAM with downloading material from sequential memory. They risk missing what is actually going on in the room.

Those who are fully present, and who are responding intuitively, are freeing up loads of megabytes to watch, feel, listen, observe, and take in everything that is really going on, as well as actually presenting their case.

Walk Outs: You have to walk away, regretfully, when despite being mindful of all of the above, the other side is persistently obstructionist, blocking your every move, resisting every suggestion, and clearly not willing or able to work towards a resolution.

And this is where the BATNA is again invaluable. You went into the room hoping for a good resolution, but knowing that you had an alternative if all failed.

But going on the basis that every single thing is negotiable, the walk away, of itself, can be an opportunity for further negotiation – unless you really, really want to slam the door to make a big point!

There is far more to be gained by defusing the tension, as the meeting ends, to allow the possibility of resuming in a few days when people have had time to think, or positions have shifted.

You might say: "So we are clearly not going to reach agreement today, but before we leave, can we discuss some options on how we might resume discussions in time?"

If options can be listed, and discussed, there is a possibility that the best option can be converted into a genuine alternative.

There is a major retail group which conducts its business along, let's say, old fashioned lines. Becoming a buyer there is a legendary training ground, and working on the shop floor fairly testing. If you can survive the jumped up managers in cheap suits, and the regular public dressing downs they love to mete out, you can survive anything.

A client of ours who provides insurance to the company described the negotiations they have once a year to get the repeat business.

"You would wonder what century they think they are in", he says. "In the middle of every negotiation they storm out in a flurry, which we now know after a number of years of doing business with them, is a complete stunt.

"We have stopped getting stressed by it. We just pour some more tea for ourselves, eat a few more chocolate biscuits, and wait for them to come back."

An Early Win: So much preparation goes into a negotiation, particularly one carrying a lot of tension, there is a danger that the negotiators will miss an early win by a country mile, and talk themselves right out of it again.

Have you ever listened to a sales pitch, and decided within a minute or two that you are buying the product, only to notice that the sales person hasn't spotted the 'buy' decision on your face, and is carrying right on with the prepared spiel?

You gently interject that yes, you are quite interested in the photocopier or the flat screen, but he keeps going right along, now in full flight, loving the sound of his own voice and the wonderfully learned off and rehearsed pitch? He is happily talking himself out of the sale.

In the same way in a negotiation you approach prepped and armed to the hilt, you might be surprised by an early concession, negating the need to carry on with all your good material.

It's hard to let the good stuff go but it has to be done. You have to fold up the tent, acknowledge the win – with respect and gratitude – and move on.

I was working recently with a man in a senior role in a

technology firm who was going for a major promotion that would have seen him reporting directly to the CEO. The company took the process very seriously and put him through about five rounds of really tense interviewing, involving the international board and other stakeholders.

For every phase of the process, my client put in huge amounts of work, coming through with flying colours, even if it felt like doing a few bouts with a prize fighter. Then it came to the final round when he had to present to the CEO and we worked hard on a great presentation concentrating solely on his vision for the role.

He arrived into the office of the CEO, laptop under his arm, fired up to do the best song and dance act of his life, and the CEO shook his hand and said: "Congratulations, I know you are going to do a great job. Will we go and have a spot of lunch?"

My client said it took a fair few minutes for him to close his mouth and to move on from the reality that his whizz, bang, wallop presentation was not required, and to enjoy the lunch that followed along with a relaxed and very general conversation with the CEO.

Choosing the Location

The big question is, does playing at home give you an advantage and does playing away hamper you? Of course the answer is yes to both. But the choice of location for a tense negotiation is not always yours to make, so you have to make do with what you have.

When I work with clients preparing for a radio or television interview, I remind them that they know their story inside out and back to front, as they speak about this stuff every day, but the environment they will be in is strange and new and that can affect how they perform when the red light goes on.

The interviewer at the other side of the TV studio or radio desk is in his or her living room, that warm cozy place they go to every day to do a job they love, surrounded by pleasant colleagues and friends. It is a huge advantage.

You can't move the furniture or sit in a different place in a broadcast studio, but you most certainly can, and probably should, when you arrive at the negotiation venue. Feeling comfortable and in full sight of the room is very important, so you should make it your business to arrive early and get things set up in a way that will work for you.

If a neutral venue is a possibility, go for it. Firstly it levels the playing field but it also offers a better opportunity to do a recce the day before, and get comfortable with the space and how your voice sounds in the room.

During the Negotiation

The best negotiations happen when both sides understand the principles and best practices we have been discussing here, but life, as we know, is not always like that. All we can do is hope that, during the reach-out prior to the negotiation, you have indicated how you intend to proceed, and that the other side will reciprocate with the same degree of civility and respect.

Wise outcomes are achieved when both sides have:

- Prepared and have done their homework well
- Collaborated on an agenda
- Picked a neutral venue
- Accepted that trust and respect is a foregone conclusion
- Separated emotions from issues, and problems from personalities
- Communicated clearly
- Considered alternative positions

- Allowed time for consideration breaks
- Noted and appreciated small gains
- Chosen a good Chair who has controlled the meeting well

After the Negotiation

When you speak to negotiators about what didn't work in any exchange, they usually come back with the same things. Typically the list includes lack of courtesy, people who are unreasonable in their approach, or stances that were just too far apart to bridge.

Conor Ronan, the CEO of Ronan Group Renewables agrees that the ideal in any negotiation is to go in with an open mind, and to try to leave something behind for the other guy, while actively working on achieving your own goals.

But sometimes despite your best intentions, you are up against a hard-ball attitude from the other side from the outset, which leaves you no option but to respond in kind.

"In a recent deal I was working on, with a Project Capex of €150,000,000 the law firm on the other side came at us like a runaway train, demanding the kitchen sink. We held our ground, and we walked away with the kitchen sink and a few gold taps as well!

"It was very tense during the negotiation, and at one point we thought the whole deal might collapse, but it worked out well for us in the end."

The most common reasons for breakdown, cited by many who negotiate every day, include:

- There was a lack of clarity about what was really going on in the room
- There were loads of words spoken, but little meaning
- The positions were not clear

- There was serious tension in the room
- There was no clear agenda or the agenda kept shifting
- They weren't chairing the meeting, but they wouldn't let us chair it
- They kept playing the man, not the ball
- They got heated and personal about nothing
- We seemed to go around in circles
- There didn't seem to be any way of resolving differences

At the end of the day negotiating is probably more about getting the other person to talk, than doing the talking yourself. By showing up to a negotiation in a really positive, mindful way, relaxed in the knowledge that you have the work done, you stand to gain so much more through respectfully listening to, and acknowledging, the concerns of the other side.

This attitude will reflect strongly in your body language from the moment you walk through the door, and do more to influence the outcomes than many of the words spoken.

A friendly, attentive, pleasant, and interested demeanour does wonders to set the tone for everything that ensues, as opposed to clenched jaws, squared shoulders, and stony expressions.

Patrick Joy founding Director of Suretank, and the Ernst and Young Irish Entrepreneur of the Year, told me how, in the best deal of his career, both sides felt they came out well in the end, despite how difficult the negotiations became half way through.

"It was the sale of 67 per cent of the company to PE in 2013. I achieved 70 per cent more than expected for the existing shareholders (30 per cent more than my own minimum) whilst at the same time giving the new shareholders a deal that they were very happy with.

"The negotiations took place over two days and initially concentrated on discussions on due diligence issues, the SPA and the shareholders' agreement. The buyers then sought a significant discount from their original pre due diligence "indicative" offer that I refused to entertain and threatened to walk away.

"I realised that everything was going to plan when they quickly retreated from that position and at the end of the day we gave them a small discount and got a great deal for all involved."

◆　◆　◆

Following the negotiation, good or bad, a response has to be made capturing what occurred – a formal response to the other side, and possibly a public or media response. Where there has been collaboration prior to the negotiation, and ground rules outlined, this will have been covered, and hopefully there will not have been a walk out and a rush to get the story on the media first.

The formal response to the other side needs to capture what are the assumptions now. Are there conditions attached? Where do we go from here? Who is going to do what and by when?

A good chair will have captured these as the negotiation has been progressing, and it will be a simple enough matter to agree and issue a joint statement.

Girls, particularly, need to start negotiating early

Are women as good at negotiating as men? Apparently not. The evidence shows that women haven't been good at narrowing the pay gap or, with some notable exceptions, negotiating the steps on the greasy ladder to the top. And we all know that when they do negotiate hard, they risk a backlash.

We probably have to start the education process early,

giving young girls the tools to master negotiation skills but also to deal with the challenges around using them.

It is not a feminist rally call but simply a statement of fact to say that lots of pre-teen girls lose their self-confidence around puberty when they suddenly realise how objectified and sexualised women are in the media and in the public eye. It makes them less sure of themselves, and less sure of their voice.

As parents, teachers, educators or employers we have to be careful about our own attitudes, given that girls and young women are swamped with messages about what it means to be female. Are we adding to the notion that being 'feminine' requires a passive communication style?

We need to work with our young females on practising age appropriate negotiations early on – getting our teens to negotiate for a night out, a new outfit or the loan of the car – and encouraging them to take part in robust debates and other activities where conflict and difference of opinion is viewed as healthy.

Young women who debate very often become student representatives, broadcasters, politicians and business leaders.

Get them talking, flex the muscle!

Chapter Eight

From Commander To Coach

In this chapter, we take a look at coaching, taking many examples from the world of sport which we can apply to business, education, social entrepreneurship and anywhere else we need to lead teams to excel.

◆　　◆　　◆

I WAS asked to give a series of talks on leadership a number of years ago by Chartered Accountants Ireland, the representative and training organisation for the accountancy profession. It was a really interesting project because, while we all know how vital the financials are to any business, on your personal leadership journey you have to show more than the top of your head, crunching the numbers, if you want to succeed.

As I prepared for the talks the term 'From Commander to Coach' seemed to sum up for me the direction I wanted to go, and it is one I have used now in lots of talks to describe how leadership, and what we expect from it, has changed radically in the recent past.

So once upon a time, the commander was the all out 'Boss'. He, and it was usually a he, was to be listened to, obeyed, and followed at all costs. He stood on the prow of the ship, had the map printed somewhere inside his head, the eye glass securely in place, and he knew exactly where he was going.

Think actor Russell Crowe looking all moody and masterful in the 2003 Peter Weir movie, *Master and Commander.*

Today no one wants to follow someone blindly because he, or she, has the word 'Boss' on the door; has a fancy title, or owns a company. We want to follow someone who has a clear vision, and who communicates it well. We want to follow someone who we know, who we can see, and whose values are aligned with our own.

The definition of misery in the workplace must be staying in a job where you really, really can't stand what the organisation or its leaders represent. Today, we all want to work in a company led by a coach, and in a department led by a coach.

You know the kind of department I am talking about – the one where people are always peering over the partitions as they walk by, because there is always such a buzz going on. Laughter emerges a lot, people are happy, they produce great results. You can be sure there is a performing leader in there somewhere.

But what is a coach, and how do you become one? How do you start developing the right attributes if you have, in the past, been more inclined to be a commander – because that seemed to be what was expected in the organisation you were in? Or if you are just starting out on the path to leadership?

Entrepreneur, Safa Sharif, Director of the Masy Holdings construction company in Bahrain, is honest enough to voice his reservations about coaching.

"I don't enjoy it as I feel impatient, as it drains me, but I do it all the time because I know it is such an important tool to let me know people better, and to enhance the relationship. I dig deep and ask a lot of 'why' questions, always trying to narrow the problem or get closer to the roots of it, and then I end by highlighting the positives."

Safa has hit there on the main problem with coaching – it takes time, patience, energy and commitment. It is so much easier to snap an instruction, or to think 'I'd be quicker doing it myself.'

They say that as a leader or owner of an organisation, you should make a list of the things you hate doing, and the things you are really bad at doing, and hire people to do those things.

This self-awareness is a big part of becoming a successful coach, according to Michael O'Leary of HRM, who enjoys coaching and has always made it central to how he runs his company.

"It works extremely well in my current team, where each member has a core strength that I don't possess at the same level, and which reflects their area of strategic responsibility. My role is to help them place it into a context which connects with other people's strategic areas, and with the longer term vision for the business."

The Leader of Today – the Coaching Pyramid

The pyramid is often used as a simple visual metaphor for the coaching process, and there are many varieties of it out there, but this is my personal favourite, which describes the attributes a coach should have or strive for.

Remembered with the acronym RICE, the coach is Rigorous, Intuitive, Caring, Engaged.

Rigorous – A coach has to have intellectual, ethical and moral rigour. You have to be what you want others to be. You won't get away with the lines we all hear ourselves using on our kids, "Do as I say, not as I do". Or even worse, "Because I said so!" You have to live every day a value system that is true, recognisable and understandable.

Intuitive – A coach has to have a big overarching vision that others buy into; an intuition about what is going to work for the team and how they are going to get there. If you want to be a real leader you have to know instinctively how to get others on board, show them their part in the whole and help them to be better than they ever thought they could be.

Caring – A coach is aware of the full human dimension of each member of the team. People don't show up to work as marketing executives, or teachers, or shop assistants in isolation. They are parents, sisters, sons, partners, dog owners, runners, bakers, gardeners, singers and all kinds of other fascinating, interesting and demanding things. You should know this.

Engaged – A coach is mindful and present when with the team. You need to put the mobile on silent, turn off your screen and give your complete attention to the person you are talking to. That means eye contact and highly developed listening skills.

Sport features largely in my world because I live in a house full of men who spend whole chunks of their lives shouting at games on the television. My three sons have been very lucky to get the best possible rugby coaching over the years, firstly at our local club and later at secondary school.

They were never first team players but I am convinced they could referee an international game in a heartbeat, or sit in to the hot seat if a TV pundit went sick, such is their technical knowledge of the game. And their deep understanding of the art of coaching.

They know that the sports coach has the vision, translates it into a strategy, makes the players believe they can do it, and gets them physically and emotionally into shape for the tournament. The coach organises them, teaches them, criticises them, praises them, motivates them and knocks the best possible tune out of them on the day.

The coach knows that in the moment, each player has to instinctively react to adversity and take advantage of opportunity, resulting sometimes in those magic moments in sport that are talked about for generations.

The Irish and English rugby teams were meeting in the third game of the Six Nations series at the Aviva Stadium in Dublin. It was a clash of giants between two unbeaten teams, who were very closely matched and where there was only ever going to be one moment or score that would make the difference.

Early in the second-half, the Irish team, which had dominated play throughout, was pressurising the English line and lured the visitors into an offside trap. The referee signalled a penalty but played advantage. Then scrum half, Conor Murray, retrieving the ball from the ruck with his left hand, gave a small signal with his right hand – captured by the TV camera crew – that he was going to box kick the ball high into the goal-line area.

Before he had put his boot near the ball, the number 12, Rob Henshaw, was already moving at speed and was in the air to collect as the inch perfect Garryowen fell from the sky.

The young centre rotated in the air, and touched the ball down behind the line for a spectacular try, the only one of the game, which left England trailing by 16 points and was instrumental in giving the home team victory on the day by 19 -9, and later the Six Nations Championship.

It was a pivotal moment in the game and watching it on the day, you knew you were seeing coaching at its very best, the Irish team delivering so ably under the skilled stewardship of Joe Schmidt.

Interestingly for me and my work, one of Schmidt's key talents is as a communicator. He is a lovely speaker, much in demand on the after-dinner circuit, with an amazing ability to explain those complex moves and game plans to a non-rugby audience. I can only imagine how good he is in the dressing-room at half-time, inspiring the team to even greater heights, a true performing leader.

So as someone interested in leadership, what can you take from the sports coach to apply to your own life and business? I think these are the things that cross over, the content and order of priority influenced by my home bred, rugby-mad focus group.

The Coach

1. Sets expectations: A good coach sets the bar high and reminds players every single day just where the bar is. He expects every member of the team to give of their best at all times, on and off the pitch. He sets and expects the highest of standards in terms of trust and respect, and never blurs the line for 'star' performers, or high-ticket players. He expects players to accept responsibility for all of their actions, and to contribute to the team in every way they know how. He ensures that each member of the team knows his individual strengths, and how they impact on the group as a whole.

2. Transfers knowledge: He uses his own in-depth and detailed knowledge of the field to teach and communicate all the bases from physical training, diet and nutrition right up to high level strategy, tactics and leadership. He has time for each individual member of the panel, knows what is going on in their world, and has a strategy in place for identifying and maximising strengths and equally identifying and minimising weaknesses.

3. Grows teams and leadership: He knows how to develop leadership within the team, growing talent not only in the sport itself but also in the running of it. Everyone knows that a strong team can achieve anything, but the good coach takes the long-term view, going after the current championship with intense focus while also protecting the pipeline. He builds a rock solid team dynamic, where players instinctively support each other and have each other's back, and grow apace in skill and character, ready to lead when their turn comes.

4. Extracts the best: He balances coaching the team as a unit with individually developing players' skills, always knowing where the extra ounce is to be found. He knows how far to push a player to get that unbelievable achievement, the one that was beyond personal expectations, but equally knows when to pull back and give a player some space. He manages expectations.

5. Manages talent: He has great self-belief and confidence and imbues his players with the same thing. He uses his experience and gut instinct to make tough decisions about who to pick and who to leave on the bench. He knows what his team needs at any time and when he hasn't got it at home, goes out and finds it. He communicates the vision of the team with potential recruits, and persuades them to come on board because of what can be achieved and the role the recruit will play in bringing the team to greatness. He wins over the recruit, closes the deal, brings him over the line and makes him feel part of the set-up so he can integrate quickly.

6. Inspires: He is able to block out negativity and criticism, and knows how to dig deep and find focus in the face of extreme adversity. When the odds are stacked against the team, he communicates hope and purpose to allow them to find a solution. He never accepts the game is over until the final whistle and lets the team know he believes in them right to the last second. He makes individuals and teams believe in themselves.

7. Listens: He knows to ask for insights, understanding that the game often feels very different from the inside. He hears what the players have to say with an open mind, using the information to inform the next game plan. He doesn't allow his personal confidence and self-belief to turn into intransigence or a reluctance to learn. His door is always open.

8. Delegates: He gives responsibilities to others, allowing them to develop as leaders. He sets tasks that will encourage their creativity to emerge and allows them to shine, which in turn fosters a willingness for other team members to step up when the opportunity arises.

9. Critiques: He knows how and when to give feedback, understanding that a player might not be at his most receptive sitting on the dressing-room bench after a disastrous game, his shoulders bowed and his head is in hands. A good coach knows that timing and tone is everything and doesn't cross the line and damage a player's confidence. But he is honest, and gives a direct, non-emotive and clinical appraisal of performance when the time is right. And he always remembers to praise when praise is due.

10. Leads: He gives example, knowing that all good leadership starts with the self.

From all of the above, we can take quite a few things into our lives as leaders of self, families, businesses and communities.

We might imagine there is a whole lot of shouting and roaring going on in the dressing-room after a game but in reality we know that the commander barking orders is dead and gone and that the only kind of leader who will thrive today, and be respected by others, is one who coaches teams to find solutions.

Here's why.

The march of technology has meant that the stock in trade of the commander, the map of the world, is out of date, yellow and curling at the edges. The person with 'Boss' on the door no longer has all the answers. The geeky kid who joined the company last Friday may be the next Mark Zuckerberg, so we had better have a little respect for him and pay attention to what he says. Organisations are flattening.

Also, we know that we are making the technology stuff up as we go along and that it is changing at the speed of light. So we need to be led by coaches who know how to bring out the best in the team and who will encourage everyone to contribute fully, in case we miss a trick and our competitors steal a march on us.

The difficult bit is that the traditional school and college system does not necessarily prepare young people to take part fully and contribute in the way I am describing. And many employers are fixated with training in technology and digital media, something we are already attracted to like a bunch of paper clips to a magnet, when they should be training for the kind of skills that encourage emotional and mental agility.

Sir Ken Robinson in his much-viewed TED talk describes how the whole education system in the western world was based on the industrial society. Students sat in straight rows, were obedient, compliant, non-questioning, non-creative, preparing themselves for a workplace led by a commander.

The argument is that the points and exam driven system, still largely favoured, produces young people who go into the work place waiting to be told what to do. We have all met them. They have all the qualifications and the technical or digital knowledge in the world, but no notion how to apply it to the workplace of today.

In much the same vein Seth Godin, in his position paper *Stop Stealing Dreams*, describes teachers of old as gamekeepers – guardians of knowledge – which they would dispense in small chunks to compliant students.

But with all the information now accessible online, the digital natives, as academic Marc Prensky first described them, can access the information much faster than the teacher can.

So today the person at the top of the room must be a teacher coach, inspiring the student to want to find the information; and must confidently encourage challenging questions, teamwork and the kind of classroom atmosphere that will nurture creativity and leadership – the essential skills for the modern age.

What scares traditional teachers most about this is the noise levels. School inspectors used to judge the competence of the teacher by the silence of the room. But we now know that it is in groups and pairs where the creative spark emerges, where the assumptions are challenged, where progress is made.

This is the kind of classroom that will produce 'think on your feet', 'take challenges face on', and 'make it up because there is no map' young people for the rapidly changing digital age. It will be noisy and interactive, with work going on in small groups, where leadership and creativity muscles are being flexed from a young age.

This is the kind of classroom that will produce the public leaders and entrepreneurs of the next generation, but also the corporate leaders because they will be intrapreneurs, who will navigate the corporate world far more effectively.

A group of educators, concerned about these notions, visited an education minister some time ago, and while he received them warmly, he told them that he did not have a budget for entrepreneurship training in the classroom, and finished by saying it is not really that important anyway. Clearly, education sometimes has to begin at the top.

The minister was obviously locked into the out-dated notion that entrepreneurship training is about teaching new venture creation only and that it is more properly a part of a business studies module or course. The opposite is actually the case – entrepreneurship training is life training.

Recently in Denmark there was a study where they taught entrepreneurship in the broadest sense to primary school children. The kids who took part showed notably better attitude, attendance, ambition and performance levels than those who did not. And the effects of the training spilled over into their home and personal lives, where they showed better use of spare time and better organisational ability.

The children also said they enjoyed school more, felt more connected and more supported by their teachers. And an education minister says this is not important?

Third-level colleges with switched-on teaching staff now know that entrepreneurial training is behaviour based, and should be integrated right across the faculties and available not just to business students but to kids of all ability levels and interests.

They are designing programmes that are based on developing confidence, determination, creativity and passion, with the hope of producing business and political leaders and social entrepreneurs who will actually try to change the world.

Teachers running those kind of classes are seeing students vote with their feet, turning up voluntarily for entrepreneurship electives and, very encouragingly – given the low numbers of women in entrepreneurship worldwide – they are seeing a big take-up from female students.

Thomas Cooney, Professor of Entrepreneurship at Dublin Institute of Technology says:

"Until such time as government officials, policy-makers and educational management recognise that entrepreneurial behaviour is not a capitalist activity, but a way of thinking and behaving, then no progress will be made towards ensuring that every child in every school receives entrepreneurship education.

"The fantastic attribute of entrepreneurship education is that the age and intellectual capacity of a student are irrelevant since engendering the ability to think positively, seek out opportunities, gather resources, build a team and add value are life-long pursuits and can be used in any context of one's life.

"Entrepreneurship education enables a person to develop their own futures and to contribute to the economic, social and artistic capital of their families, communities and countries. How can anybody possibly have a difficulty with such an outcome?"

Governments need to wake up to this kind of thinking, and they need to assign the budgets to equip our young people for the world of work of the future.

But back to you as a coach leader, what are the markers you should think about when hiring young people to join the team, to see if they have developed the kind of critical thinking and mental attitudes that will allow them to thrive?

And if you spot the potential, how will you then develop and encourage those skills?

The top markers for me are:

The ability to make choices: Their love of technology can allow them to exercise nothing but their thumbs, shooting aliens in their bedrooms on gaming consoles or to explore, access and appreciate the wonder and the power of information available in a way that was never there before.

Analysis and good judgment: The societal parameters laid down by the institutions like churches, states, and banks have been tarnished. Personal integrity is all we have left. Are their values aligned with yours?

Problem solving: It takes confidence and skill to believe that whatever befalls us, whatever is in store for us, we have the intellectual rigour and the resilience to find a way around it. What personal problems have they faced and solved?

Willingness to fail: Do they know how many failures it takes to get a win. Will they fall apart if they do fail, or learn and move on?

Leadership: Not based on title, years on the job, or pay grade but based on belief, insight and passion for the project. What projects have they led to completion?

Creativity: The ability to take away the barriers of judgment, bias and insecurity, and to let all the ideas in to the silo. Are they open to new ideas?

The confidence to dream: And to persuade others to believe in the vision and get on board.

The ability to communicate: None of the above is of any real use if it can't be communicated.

So much of it comes down to how we communicate, or perform on a day to day basis. And how mindful we are of our impact on others.

A report from the Harvard Business School on the future of the MBA has identified that completing students often lack an awareness of their impact on others, and show a requirement for work in the area of personal skills and the practice of leadership.

It is all about connecting with our fellow human beings and understanding and being understood in real time, not in virtual time. The connector is human emotion. And we have to find the confidence to use this emotion in our personal communication in business, in order that we will reach people, connect with them and get them to come on our journey with us.

Yes, it is always argued that there is no room for emotion in business – feelings should be left at the far side of the door – and certainly we can all do without high drama and emotional strops in the workplace. But there is room, and indeed a serious need, for emotional connection in the workplace.

The thing that strikes you most about successful entrepreneurs is their belief in, and absolute passion for, their product or service. Money or acclaim are secondary drivers. The prime driver inevitably is the belief that the world really, really, needs the product or service.

Entrepreneur Noelle O'Connor is the founder of the tanning product TanOrganic. Listening to her speak at an event one time, I heard her describe how women went to great lengths to eat healthily, when everything you ingest that way is filtered by the liver before it gets to the blood stream.

Yet they put tanning lotions all over the skin, which is the largest body organ and the one without a filter, sending the ingredients straight to the blood stream, without first checking what is in the bottle.

She couldn't sleep knowing that we could be destroying our health, and set about developing a tanning product that is completely safe. She came up with the world's first fully certified organic tan.

And that is what we are looking for in training and education in the workplace. We are looking to develop people who have an emotional connection with what they are doing – because that is the true genesis of confidence, creativity, leadership and all of the above. Imagine just how much better prepared for our new work environment those young people would be, if throughout their school and college training, they had to present, argue, negotiate, pitch and emotionally connect with, and believe in, and care about a subject – every time they wrote a paper? Instead of just reproducing dry facts to gain a high mark?

As a coach your role is to seek out and find the right people for your team, and when you have them in place, to train them to be the best they can be, bringing in outside resources as appropriate. Your role is also about being crucially aware of your own style and behaviours and how they impact on others.

The Art of Feedback

As a coach leader, giving feedback will be a big part of your job. And of course the converse is equally valid, taking it. Because that is when the real lines of communication open up.

Giving feedback means telling a co-worker about the effect their work style, performance or behaviour is having on the team and its output and dynamic.

Feedback can be shared up, down or across an organisation. It can build good relationships and get everyone working together to achieve team goals. It can also help individuals re-boot their performance and increase their personal effectiveness and job satisfaction.

Frank Lampard, former top Chelsea FC top goal scorer tells a great story about the time manager Jose Mourinho stopped him in the shower room after a Saturday game and says, "There's something I want to talk to you about".

Jose was fully dressed, and Frank was in the altogether, so it was a little awkward, and Frank may not have been ready to listen.

But Jose went on to say that Frank was one of the best players in the world, and there wasn't a game that he saw that didn't reconfirm that belief in his mind.

Frank says that he went home floating on air, and was still floating when he arrived back in for training on the Monday morning. The power of positive feedback, despite the location!

Unfortunately a lot of people don't like giving, or getting, feedback. The giver fears hurt and rejection and the receiver feels like they are being criticised or judged.

Approached correctly, it can make a huge difference to how a team works together. When feedback follows a defined and agreed pattern, that everyone knows and uses, it can deliver great results and improve relationships enormously.

The steps below are very simple to follow and make the experience better for everyone.

The giver of feedback should:

- **Check intent:** Why am I choosing to give this feedback? Am I doing this to genuinely help this person, or is it about me asserting my authority?
- **Check time:** Is this the right time to give the feedback? Is the recipient open now to taking this on board? (And place. Not the shower room!)
- **Ask permission:** Is the recipient ok with the idea of feedback on this project in the first place?
- **Be specific:** No broad strokes. Give clear feedback on line items, not the overall project or event
- **Note the impact:** On both the giver and the receiver! How did you feel? How did he or she feel?
- **Specify how to move forward:** Clarity is everything. Agree what should be done differently in future.
- **Check for understanding:** On both sides. Is the recipient clear now on what needs to change? Are you clear on all the circumstances that led to this situation?

The receiver of feedback should:

- Release tension by asking questions. Get absolute clarity as to where the concerns are.
- Summarise the feedback. "So, you are concerned that my delay in telling you about the problems we are having with the project is causing confusion...
- Ask what the request is. How should things be done differently?
- Respond to the feedback. Accept the request, or make an alternative suggestion.

- Express understanding. Offer thanks for the feedback!

Despite the best of intentions, feedback can go pear-shaped. People go home for the weekend, fuming and worrying and taking it out on their families, and arrive back in on Monday ashen-faced and stressed. This is not what should happen and maybe Friday afternoon is not the time for the feedback session.

Following the protocols above should prevent it going wrong. Ideally, both the giver and the receiver of the feedback should feel more aligned after the session and more in agreement about where things should go in the future.

If it does go wrong, it is usually because:

- The timing was wrong
- The location was wrong – no privacy
- The language was judgmental
- Permission was not sought
- There is no organisational culture of giving and receiving feedback
- The giver or the receiver were upset or emoting
- The giver gave incomplete or non-specific feedback
- There was no direction to the feedback or specific request attached
- There was no agreement on next steps
- In the organisation, there only ever seems to be feedback on bad situations, not good ones.
- The giver did not thank the receiver for accepting the feedback
- The receiver did not thank the giver for offering the feedback

Scott McDonald, who we heard earlier brought his company back from the brink of bankruptcy, regularly uses feedback as a tool:

"I always encourage others to make mistakes, a mistake is only a mistake if we don't learn from the experience. This has helped to establish a culture of non-blame and personal growth throughout my organisation and my personal life.

"The word 'problem' is thrown out – it is an 'opportunity.' We always look at it as an opportunity for continuous improvement – a company core value – or change for the better."

♦   ♦   ♦

The workplace as we know it is changing very rapidly. There is a direct correlation between the rise of companies without tangible assets – the companies that have Intellectual Property – and the rise of the coach as the preferred style of leader.

Like the switched-on teacher or academic, the coach relies on the RICE principles – rigour, intuition, care, and engagement. And he or she has the confidence to say, I don't know the answer, let's work it out together.

In my own life, I try hard to be a coach and not a commander, but at times I fail dismally.

Like when I roar at the rugby fanatics to stop messing around with the ball, and do something useful like mowing the lawn. Because I said so!

Chapter Nine

Leadership Challenges Experienced By Women

In this chapter we explore the particular challenges that confront women when it comes to leadership and displaying executive presence; a knowledge of which will help all leaders, male and female, to understand better their own interactions and to inspire and support their teams.

♦ ♦ ♦

EVERY time I attend a glamorous women in business awards night, or women of the year lunch, my heart soars for the fantastic women being honoured, the work they are doing and the leadership they are performing.

And then I wonder, why is it necessary to award women in this way? Why have we seen more and more of these events emerge in the recent past, in a kind of loud claiming of an inherently divisive space, which we really should not need as a feature of our society.

We never hear of men in business awards nights, or men of worth lunches. Men are usually honoured in places like the worldwide Ernst and Young Entrepreneur of the Year awards, or local Chamber of Commerce events, which may be historically male dominated but are actually gender neutral, and open to all.

So why do women not show up, in equal numbers, in the early rounds of these events so that they have a chance of making it through to the final? Do they rule themselves out before the start line, putting themselves forward instead for female only competitions, where they feel they are in with a chance?

Enterprise Ireland, the business support agency, made a call-out a number of years ago for high potential start-up companies to join a competitive funded accelerator programme. They received over a hundred applications for 30 places, but were very disappointed at the number of female led business applicants, which only amounted to a handful.

The following year they advertised a similar programme for female led businesses only, and were astonished to receive 130 applicants for the programme. So where were all those businesses the first time around? Clearly out there, but not stepping forward, unless the path ahead was obviously safe and accessible.

Women are currently emerging in their thousands in the start-up space. They are proving themselves to be more entrepreneurial than was previously imagined, and are accessing supports from business development agencies in far greater numbers than men.

They are out there, working hard, more visible than ever before and actively nominating their female friends and colleagues for the aforementioned awards ceremonies.

But to really make a difference, I think we should be focusing less on rewarding individual women. What we really need is a major worldwide award scheme, on a par with the Ernst and Youngs, that recognises and rewards companies and organisations that are truly tackling diversity and inclusivity, and can show the numbers to back up what they are doing.

Because top down change has to occur to meet and greet determination from the ranks – women who are prepared to take charge of their careers, and develop themselves to take on the challenges of leadership. It has been proven time and again that organisations with a higher proportion of women leaders perform better. This is the business case for gender diversity, not the warm and fluffy stuff about 'wouldn't it be nice' to have more women at senior management level or on the board.

Study after study from research organisations like Catalyst, Davys, Deloitte and Forbes have shown that the bottom line improves in direct proportion to the numbers of women in these positions.

Diversity is good for business, and good for all of us, and yet the gender gap persists.

UK *Dragon* investor Hilary Devey presented a two-part documentary for the BBC called *Women on Top*, a look at how women in Britain are turning up in the workforce. The programme found that in the companies they surveyed men held 70 per cent of middle management jobs, and a massive 84 per cent of senior and boardroom jobs.

They conducted a number of exercises with the participating companies, finding that teams that had gender balance seriously outperformed those which were predominantly single sex. In a nice twist at the end, Hilary found that in her own company, Pall-Ex, the most profitable department was the one that had a 50/50 gender balance.

It is often argued that 30 per cent is the tipping point – that place where, once achieved, the true benefits of diversity can kick in, changing organisational culture and even the goals and direction of any given concern. Achieving the 30 per cent target requires a female workforce that is willing to take on leadership, and a male workforce willing to embrace and even become advocates for the positive change that will ensue.

So if you are a woman, you have to want to progress. You have to own your ambition, and hang on to it throughout – and despite – the stages of life you are likely to go through; pregnancy, young children, teens, elder parent care and so on.

And as a man, you have to ask yourself this. Do you become resentful at the way women (like me!) bang on about this stuff, or do you want to see equality in the workplace, and everywhere else, simply because it is fair and right?

Do you think it is something you can contribute to yourself? If it is within your remit to support and promote your female workforce, why wouldn't you do it? Given the worldwide leadership shortage we discussed earlier, and the benefits to all from a happy and healthy workplace.

The stumbling blocks to female advancement are similar whether in business, politics, or society in general and they include the personal factors of confidence, ambition, and motivation and the external factors of opportunity and stereotyping. Outright or obvious discrimination would seem to be less of an issue than it used to be, at least in the developed world.

In a series of focus groups I conducted recently on gender diversity with the senior female staff members of a financial institution, some really interesting findings emerged around this subject. There was complete agreement that there was no actual glass ceiling, that any woman who had a strong desire to progress would do so.

However, they also agreed that women were not progressing to senior roles as frequently as men did, because of the career choices they made. And these career choices were influenced by a perceived lack of flexibility at the most senior levels, and a perceived inability to carry forward hard-fought-for special hours or work arrangements to a higher level.

So one of the reasons why women would not put themselves

forward for a promotion they were well qualified for was the fear of losing a flexible work pattern, which was crucial to their family arrangements.

One respondent, who did not herself have children, and had never availed of unusual hours, said that flexible arrangements were clearly of benefit to the whole organisation, not just the person who applied for them. She said it was a clear way to maintain highly-trained staff within the organisation and to maintain a happy and productive workforce.

The whole group agreed the system allowed continuity in a career – a time to step back slightly when that was required and equally an opportunity to step forward again. They said that flexible arrangements, which had had been introduced in the 1990s, had been key to the emergence of women within the organisation, and the reason why they currently figured in good numbers in management roles.

The next constructive move, they felt, was to make those arrangements widely available to men also, to change it from a 'female thing' to a 'family friendly' or 'work-life balance thing' and also to level the playing field for women who work these arrangements.

They described the micro discriminations experienced by the women who worked the flexible hours. Even where it is widely known that someone is contracted to work until say, 4pm, there will be comments about 'taking a half day again' as they get ready to leave. Or where the staff member has a flexi arrangement and arrives at 10am, there is a comment like 'good of you to join us at last' from members of the team who were there earlier.

While seemingly made in jest, these comments rankled.

Women often find themselves judged in a stereotypical way, by other women as well as men. It seems to be more readily accepted that men can be complex characters with a range of different abilities and contributions to make. But women are to be categorised into stereotypes that undermine their potential and contribution.

You have heard them all before, and they are usually completely contradictory.

- She is an ice queen, or over-emotional and way out there
- She is wrapped up in her kids, or single and lonely
- She is a complete schemer, or politically inept
- She's a ball breaker, or far too girly
- She's too opinionated and ambitious, or too silent and invisible
- She's a pushover, or far too angry

Damned if she does and damned if she doesn't!

Michelle Obama was referred to as an 'angry black woman' when she first went on the US Presidential campaign trail with Barack Obama back in 2008. A Harvard-trained lawyer, with a career that had been more advanced than that of her husband, she had to deliberately soften up her words and her appearance to make herself acceptable to the wider voting public, eventually becoming better known for her fashion and her kitchen garden.

She was following right on the heels of Hilary Rodham Clinton, who carefully deleted the Rodham when she first went on the campaign trail with Bill Clinton, the campaign managers telling her that retaining her own name was off-putting to the voters.

Developing and retaining the best talent is something that every organisation wants to do, because it is the key to remaining competitive in today's world. So it behoves all of us to make sure that half the talent doesn't walk out the door because the place becomes so uncomfortable.

We can all play our part in stamping out micro discriminations and stereotyping by becoming aware of the detrimental effects of language or behaviours that are unacceptable and by actively promoting gender balance in teams and groups.

And all of this will undoubtedly help the situation, but ultimately, women who want to get on will have to consciously choose to do so. They will also have to discover and work on self-limiters, the things that prevent them from moving forward.

"I have found that men lead from the front, while women pick up on the detail from behind," a female director of a financial institution told me. "In my experience, both outside and inside the organisation I am currently in, men are quite happy to put women into that supporting role.

"But here's the thing, women are often just as happy to assume that role, offering to add value to the male colleague's offering, rather than originating a strong offering for themselves."

She went on to describe people who stand out or who emerge in her industry as having a willingness to put their necks on the block; to risk holding a particular position or view and to publicise it – chancing notice and acclaim as a result, or equally disapproval. In her experience women were less likely to take those risks.

She suggested that one reason for this is that females may be said to be exhibiting characteristics that are 'unwomanly' when they display the same behaviours that may be rewarded in men.

The self-limiters that women admit to, again and again, behind closed doors and when the chips are down, include not speaking up, blending in, lacking confidence, no role models, avoiding networking, losing purpose during maternity leave, failing to confront the problem, and failing to delegate.

So let's look at these more closely, based on my experience of working with thousands of women in business, education and entrepreneurship.

Not speaking up at meetings

Women say that male colleagues are not only willing to report up, all the way to board level, but are actively seeking opportunities to do so, in the interest of visibility and making themselves known. They notice that females at the same level report up capably and well when they are asked to do so, but the difference is they don't actively look for opportunities.

And they say that women are slow to 'own' a position, waiting to see the lie of the land before coming down on one side or the other.

"I find reporting into an agenda item at a management meeting very difficult", a senior partner in a professional services firm told me. "I usually arrive, make my report and leave. I never come early to chat or mingle, or stay afterwards to have coffee, in the way I see my male colleagues doing."

Another group of women from the marketing department in the same firm felt that they were 'creeping' in the door and slipping in to the back of the room, waiting to be pounced upon to make their report, which they would then stutter and stumble through, before sliding out of the room again.

Rudeness we can't legislate for. If the Chair of the meeting hasn't the courtesy to welcome someone into the room, indicate a seat, and tell them when the meeting will be coming to that item – that is a serious corporate culture fail, and one we won't solve here.

But in this case, we worked first on owning expertise. If you have been invited from a department, you are the expert at that moment, and you know more than the generalists at the board meeting. Know this, and enjoy delivering the information.

Then you have to own the space. You don't slide into the back of the room self-limiting your own importance. You smile, say hello, ask are they ready for you, and decide where you will make your presentation – sitting or standing, whichever is comfortable.

And if there is an opportunity to stay for the coffee, it is probably a good idea.

Women often say, they don't have time for 'office politics', preferring to get the work done well, and then to get on home. But politics as we said earlier, is simply understanding the sources and uses of power. And the offline chats, over the coffee, give you a very good insight to how that is working in your organisation.

Blending in

Women say that they get their heads down, work hard, do the job very well, and the result should speak for itself. And then they are really surprised and disappointed when they don't get put forward for the promotion, because no one knew what they had been doing.

This is a lesson I learned very early on.

After my first year in the RTÉ newsroom, preparing and reading hourly news bulletins for the music station 2FM, I decided that I was ready for more responsibility and went to a duty editor for a chat about it.

I was sure that I would get a great hearing because I had made it my business to never read the same bulletin twice, running around like a lunatic between the hours to gather new sound clips and to rewrite the copy.

I used to think it must be awful for the taxi drivers on the rank to hear the same bulletin read over and over, as often happened at the time, and that my diligence and conscientiousness would stand out.

Youthful naivety!

The editor listened to my pitch attentively and then said, "Well Orlaytthh, we'll see what we can do," in that tone that lets you know that absolutely nothing is going to be done.

And with a sinking feeling I realised that if he did not know

PERFORM AS A LEADER

how to pronounce my name, the name with which I had introduced myself at the top of every bulletin for a solid year, he had never listened to one of them! Lesson learned.

Spend 80 per cent of the time working hard, and 20 per cent telling people what you are doing. Which is about the same proportion anyone in the SME sector would apply to their business, 80% of time spent on the work and 20% on marketing and advertising.

Lacking Confidence

Women often talk about 'imposter syndrome', that sense that when you do get recognition or a promotion, you feel ill-equipped for the role, or have a feeling that you are going to be found out. It was all a mistake. Someone else should have got the job.

Up to half of women managers say that they have feelings of self-doubts about their performance and career, when only about thirty per cent of men will say the same.

A woman I have known for years has an amazing track record. First in her class throughout her college years, and then a stellar career, promotion after promotion coming her way easily and regularly. And every single time she gets a promotion, she confides, 'I'm not sure why they gave me the job, I'm sure there must have been much better candidates'.

Yes, really!

And it is also well understood that women are less likely to apply for a job in the first place, unless they can meet all, or nearly all, the requirements and competencies for the role. This compares with their male colleagues, who will 'have a go' if their experience even loosely matches the job spec.

My female banking focus groups described this as a peculiarly female trait: the sense of not stepping up without the strong possibility of success, in this case pre-evaluated by the numbers of boxes on the list of criteria that can be ticked prior to application.

If women don't present themselves for roles, they can't get them. Simple as. So team leaders need to encourage them to go forward.

No Role Models

In another financial institution where I worked with female managers recently, the issue of strong role models emerged within the group. The women managers, many of whom were in their forties, recalled starting out twenty years earlier when the only women at higher levels were notoriously tough characters, who none of the group had any aspiration to emulate.

Those women had clearly emerged from a different era, when they believed the way to get ahead was to act like men, rather than owning their difference and bringing it to the table – the very difference we now know is impacting positively on the bottom line.

The women who I met in that particular company, now know that their kind of leadership is different but equally valid, and is having an impact both up and down the organisation. They understand that they are role models, right now, to younger women, and they are beginning to get a sense that at board level they are increasingly valued, as steps are put in place to offer training and development in order to hold on to them.

They are the pool from which senior management and board level positions will be filled, and if they are not there in the first place in representative numbers, they can't possibly emerge at the top levels.

The corporate world is slowly waking up to the fact that it is no longer acceptable to have single gender boards and senior management teams, expected to represent the entire population. But it has been a long road.

EU Justice Commissioner Viviane Reding has done Trojan work in shining a spotlight on gender in the workplace issues. In

November 2012, when she succeeded in bringing a proposal before the European Parliament aiming for 40 per cent female representation on the boards of publicly quoted companies by 2020, she described it as 'the most difficult battle' of her 40-year political career.

One financial institution recently circulated a picture of the new board of directors showing three women present in the line-up. It was described by the women I met as the single strongest statement the organisation had ever made about the regard in which women are held – the picture impacting more strongly on the female work force than the organisation could ever have imagined.

Avoiding Networking

Women often say that they avoid, or are reluctant to attend networking opportunities both internal and external to their organisations for a number of reasons. Firstly, they find it hard to make the time for these events, if they are outside hours, because of their family commitments. Then they often underestimate the value of them, and finally – and this is a big one – they feel awkward and unsure about landing into them on their own and being able to break the ice or start the relevant conversations.

Networking is very important for those offline 'understanding the politics' conversations mentioned earlier, for visibility, for being seen to support the organisation, for appearing career focused and ambitious, and of course for making those essential contacts.

But it is hard, undoubtedly, until you practice it a while, and get used to it. See the box on networking for tips at the end of this chapter to make it easier.

Losing purpose during maternity leave

Maternity leave has been hard fought for and hard won, as a

civilised response to the business of bringing the next generation into the world. It is not a women's issue, it is a societal issue. Nevertheless, women are deeply conscious of the time out they take, and the impact this may have on their teams and colleagues.

Some women say they never want to be anything less than a full team member. Therefore if they have not completed their families, they do not go forward for high profile roles or promotions because of concern over letting the team down , or the possibility of others having to take on an increased workload while they are off.

They take their maternity leave allowance, and fret that on their return they will not have the same job, or the same level of responsibility, or that they will be viewed differently.

Other women view a long absence as an entitlement, and make it clear that they do not want any contact from the job. They want to focus on motherhood for the duration, without any interruptions, and that is their choice.

But more again are somewhat ambivalent. They want to give the appropriate time and concentration to something as life altering as giving birth, but they want to retain a sense of who they are, and what their capabilities and contribution into the future might be.

I remember after my first child, someone older and wiser telling me, 'you will lose yourself completely after each child, and it is very important to find yourself again.' And it was so true. You become immersed in the wonder of the new little person, and find it hard for a while to re-connect with your previous self.

But a long period without any contact at all with one's centre of professional expression is demoralising, and confidence-sapping. So how is this to be managed by HR and local managers, who may be gripped by a sort of political correctness, and are afraid to reach out to women on leave for fear of a backlash from the woman herself, the unions or other representative bodies?

One of the financial companies I mentioned earlier has come up with a handbook on best practice around this – an opt-in system where women on maternity leave can choose to receive circulars and newsletters to keep in touch, and to attend the odd team briefing or meeting as they ready themselves to return to work.

The incidence of women returning to work, and continuing to play a full role, is likely to increase substantially if they feel involved in this way, and more importantly, a valued member of the team who management clearly want to hold on to.

Failing to Confront the Problem

Women often push problems to one side, rather than dealing with them head on. Problems shelved in this way fester, and can lead to all kinds of rumour and conjecture which is ultimately demoralising to everyone. Or they can over-talk the problem, and allow it to go around and around the houses, with everyone having a say in what should be done.

Performing leaders need a problem-ometer in their kit bag – a way of instantly measuring the seriousness of the issue in order to respond accordingly with due empathy and attention, and an agreed timeframe for the definitive decision. This is not to be mistaken for an instant knee-jerk or impulsive reaction, but is rather a practised and studied style of response that suggests strength and direction.

It is people-centred, and acknowledges that when someone presents with a problem, it really is a problem – either to them personally or to the organisation. They need eye contact, and mindfulness, if only for a few minutes, to validate their concerns and to let them know that the issue will be dealt with in due course.

Failing to Delegate

We discussed earlier the issue of getting the head down, and the work will speak for itself. In the same way, women often do all the work themselves, because they honestly believe it is easier than taking the time to explain to someone else how to do it. Then they leave themselves so exhausted and worn out that when they do, finally, pass something on, they snap the head off the colleague involved and reinforce a stereotype.

In leadership terms, women have to realise that doing it all themselves is not the answer; that they do not have to prove themselves over and over again by the impossible volume of work they try to take on; that if they want to be really impressive they will learn to delegate.

A woman I have recently begun coaching on communication and performance often complains of how work is landed on her desk late in the day. She thinks it is because they know she is single, does not have family commitments, and will stay on late into the evening to get it finished.

This is her pattern, and this is exactly what she does. She stays late until the work is done, missing her gym work, her choir, and her social life, which is actually very good, but all the while resenting that she is the one who is always asked.

She is her own worst enemy. Part of her is flattered to be asked, and thinks that yes, she is the only one who could turn the work around in the time involved. She has a team who work with her, any one of whom could technically do the work, but the trouble is she does not trust them to do it as well as she can do it herself.

But the only way they will ever learn is by doing the work, less well at first, but better as they get some practice. And my client's immediate boss, currently happily landing work on her desk late, knowing it will be done, needs to realise that she is not always available, and by leaving it to the last minute, may get work back to a different standard.

Finding the Inner Entrepreneur

With the best will in the world, many women will jump over the corporate wall and out into the great unknown – because of those family commitments, or because of a sense that there is a lot more to be done, and possibly more room for personal development and work life balance out there.

The world of entrepreneurship takes very well to corporate refugees, who bring with them all of the structures and discipline they have learned while navigating the highly competitive world they have recently inhabited. Add to that some resilience, creativity and performing leadership skills, and there is high possibility of success.

Women are poised to make a big impact on entrepreneurship in the coming years, increasing the numbers from where they currently stand at about 12% in the developed world.

Paula Fitzsimons is the founder of Going for Growth and the national coordinator of the Global Entrepreneurship Monitor. She tells me she is really engaged with the impact women have been making in this area.

"There are now almost 1,000 women a month setting up new businesses in Ireland. That may seem like a lot of new businesses. But if women were setting up new businesses at the same rate as men, there would be many more new businesses being started in Ireland each year.

"The challenge now is not only about getting more women active as entrepreneurs, it is about ensuring that the maximum number of new and established businesses, which are owned by women, can survive and grow".

Her view is shared by Olwen Dawe who runs Irish Business Intelligence and mentors for growth.

"Traditionally, we've seen a notable absence of women at the helm of businesses and start-ups, but this is changing. Women bring a very different tone and focus to business; their natural bent towards collaboration, reflection and risk-aversion provides balance and clarity.

"There's a long-running joke that if Lehman Brothers had been Lehman Sisters, things might have been quite different in the world. Role models are key, so the more women we see in senior management or entrepreneurial positions – the more women will pursue these roles. You can't be what you can't see"

♦   ♦   ♦

Ultimately, career momentum for women comes down to two things – personal drivers and social awareness around a certain kind of thinking and behaviours.

For women, making a series of small adjustments in how they perform could hugely improve how confident and effective they come across, and more importantly, how they feel. One of these adjustments has to be setting out to acquire top level communications skills – the skills to negotiate the deal, persuade and influence others, shine at meetings, coach teams and get the vision across on a public platform.

Whatever way we look at it, the business environment is still essentially male dominated and women, like any other minority, have to do more to stand out. Doing more means working harder and smarter and performing at a higher level. Average is not enough, because it will be perceived as underperforming.

And this is back to damned if you do and damned if you don't!

An ordinary, solid level of output will be read as not really enough, while over performing, which I am suggesting is what may well be required, will threaten those around you, women as well as men.

A highly developed set of communication skills is the only answer, to achieve the right level of visibility without coming across as intimidating or a ball-breaker – another stereotype!

How to Network

You leave the office late and arrive into a sea of faces in the function room, everyone standing around chatting up a storm, and you can't see a single person you know. So you make a beeline for the toilet, re-apply the lipstick, or adjust the tie, hum a little bit, and come back out to try again.

Still no joy, and you are just beginning to feel awkward, when you spot boring Johnny from accounts propping up the wall. Not exactly who you came here to meet, but he'll have to do.

But four and a half minutes is just about all you can take on his holidays in Benidorm, and you have no idea how to get out of this, without being horribly rude.

Sound familiar?

Networking is an important part of career progression for everyone and it is easier than it looks. But people are put off engaging by a sense of awkwardness and it can become a self limiter. Here are a few ideas to help.

At every event, everyone else is there for the same reason, to meet people! The main barrier to that happening is the one you create yourself – the barrier of the hesitant step, the uncertain look and the deflated demeanour.

Remember that the shortest distance between two people is a smile, and yours is probably a cracker. So get the head up, the shoulders back and enter the room with a flourish, megawatt smile firmly in place. Pause to have a good scan of the room, and to allow people see you, and then head straight for an open group and join in.

And how do you know an open group? Well, colleagues or a tight group of friends will be standing close together, facing into the group fully, their heads leaning slightly towards the middle. An open group, or one that has just assembled in the last few minutes, will be standing a little further apart from each other, with their bodies slightly to one side, and their heads further apart.

You can join these groups with ease once you crash-land right on in, and don't hover.

People who hover at the edge of a group, neither in nor out, look strange. A group noticing someone like this may do the decent thing and invite the stranger in, but they are just as likely to begin to close up the group, in a completely subconscious circling of the wagons. We have been warned for years not to talk to strangers!

But someone who lands right in to the middle of the group with something interesting to say will be warmly welcomed. He acts like a long lost cousin, and immediately everyone begins to treat him like one.

Open questions are best, things that give people somewhere to go and a chance to avoid the dreaded 'Did you have trouble parking the car?' conversation.

These are some of the suggestions that have been made by participants on our networking seminars who want to get the conversational ball rolling, without trying to be too clever!

- So what is waiting for you when you get back to your desk?
- Are you feeling the recovery in your industry?
- How many balls have you in the air at the moment?
- Are you looking forward to the talk/show/conference?
- Was it a hassle making the time to get here today?

This kind of question gives the person you are talking to a chance to share some information about themselves, their work, or even their home lives, and give you the opportunity to connect on a personal level, which is what networking is all about.

So, during the course of the conversation you have expertly started, you are working on obtaining:

Name
Fame
Game
· **Same**

You are trying to get the person's name – and retain it! – find out what their passion is, what their profession is, and what you have in common with them.

Passions range from golf to shopping to books (women have to be careful about talking about the kids!) and they are a great leveller and a great connector. We can talk for ages about these things, and then remember much later that we were supposed to be 'networking'. But the conversation will have been real, and very connected, and could be the basis for a strong and long-term business relationship.

At the end of such a pleasant, personal conversation, a business card will go down like a lead balloon, so instead offer to do something for your new associate arising out of the conversation. Offer to send them the email address of that person who might be able to help them, the title of that book you were referring to, the name of the doctor who was so good, the hockey coach who might help the child, and so on.

You now have an opportunity to follow up and, when the time is right, suggest a meeting about your business proposition.

Finally, to get out of the conversation and move on around the room, don't ever use the horrible expression 'must mingle now', which tells your companion loudly that he is boring/of no use as a contact/keeping you from talking to the really interesting people. Instead, shift position slightly, bring someone new into the group, or join forces with the group next door, do the introductions and move on naturally in the position shuffle that follows.

Chapter Ten

Turning Up The Dial

Finally, I want to share with you a few ideas on motivation, the things that get us out of bed in the morning, keep us going when things are tough, and make us stay focused on all the wonderful possibilities yet to come.

◆　　◆　　◆

BECOMING a performing leader is a challenge – yet another bar to clear when you have so many out there in front of you already. But of all the goals you might set yourself, the ones we have talked about here are probably the most achievable, and definitely completely within your own control.

These are ones you can start working on whenever you are ready, putting simple techniques into place and quickly getting results.

But to get going on your plan, you have to think about what inspires you. What drives you to put in that extra effort.

Virgin Group founder, Richard Branson, wrote recently as part of a motivation question put out by social media platform LinkedIn: "My professional inspiration has no separation from my personal inspiration: It is the people who will stop at nothing to make a positive difference to other people's lives. I am fortunate to come across quite a few of these game-changing people, and the desire to help (and keep up with them!) is what drives me."

I thought it very interesting that a man with Branson's profile and track record – to whom, no doubt, thousands of people look to every day for direction – finds his own motivation from people he meets who want to give back or make a difference. And he has the humility to say that he is trying to keep up with those people, not the other way around.

Some of the leaders who contributed to this book had other interesting things to say about finding personal motivation.

Brian MacCraith, the President of Dublin City University, put it in the context of winter training on mucky nights, or visits to the dentist. "You know you have to go through it, but you're thinking of the big picture all the time. And what drives me in leadership is transformation, so that you can, by working through what you have to work through, the granular detail, make significant things happen.

"I'll be measured on where I brought the university to, but I'm much less concerned about my personal reputation in that regard, as about transforming lives. The title of my strategic plan is Tranforming Lives in Societies and it is about transforming the lives of our students so that we give them a platform in life that is always adapting to the outside world. So we're giving them the springboard to flourish in society, and flourish in their private lives, and particularly flourish in the workplace.

"I think I'm driven by strategic intent. That's the satisfaction of leadership as far as I'm concerned."

Leonard Moloney, SJ, described the motivation he receives from a regular meeting of other principals, in an informal set-up very similar to the Forum process I referred to earlier in the book and which I'll describe shortly.

"Twice a year, a number of heads plus another Jesuit, we meet normally down in Spanish point, from a Wednesday evening through to Friday lunchtime. The Wednesday evening is just letting our hair down, and the Thursday takes a terrific format. It's very simple. Each one of us given the conch if you like, to take as much time as we want to talk about our experience since last we've met, or even beyond that.

"And we just talk through everything, all concerns. And over the years it has morphed as well into being very personal for a lot of us, and people give significant feedback. It is so supportive."

So how do we start turning up the dial in our own lives and worlds, finding the ways to shake ourselves out of the lethargy that sometimes makes us feel like we are wearing concrete boots?

Writers will always tell you that they have to change their environment when they get stuck. Staring at the computer won't clear the logjam but going for a walk or climbing a mountain just might do the trick. The inspiration they are looking for is then triggered by a random encounter with another walker, or a spectacular view, or simply by getting the blood flowing and allowing a re-oxygenated brain to do its job.

At a media leadership programme I attended in Cape Town a few years back, called the Entertainment Masterclass, I first heard the theory of the Cybernetic Loop and it was so impactful.

Former comedian Paul Boross, now a successful author and business coach, came bounding into the training room and shook up our thinking with his energy and vitality. I know I wasn't the only one who took it fully on board, and have been living it ever since.

"I first discovered the idea of the cybernetic loop as a performer at The Comedy Store in London," he recalls. "It is renowned as the toughest place for comedians in the UK to perform because the audience are encouraged to heckle and harass the performers. I noticed that comedians (including many who went on to become household names) could control the chances of them winning the audience over merely by how they prepared their physiology backstage.

"Comedians who stood up straight with shoulders back as they were about to go on stage automatically acted more confidently, took control and won respect from the crowd.

"I found that if I kept a good posture, lifted my chin and smiled, even though I was scared inside, it changed the way I thought about the whole performance. As I walked onto stage like a gladiator entering the ring, I felt an inward calmness and I found myself more able to tame the baying crowd.

"I realised that my physiology had a massive impact on my psychology and started to develop the technique so that I could not only use it to change my own feelings and perceptions, but also to help other people control theirs."

Ninety five per cent of your emotions – both positive and negative – are influenced by how you talk to yourself, the little voice in your head that tells you that you are going to be great, or the one that keeps telling you that you are going to crash and burn.

So it's not the things that happen to you but the way you interpret these events, and what you tell yourself about them, that determine how you feel at any given time. Then, how you feel completely influences how you respond, and what your body language is saying loudly to all those around you.

If you are sitting in a slump, feeling sorry for yourself, mentally exhausted, you need to physically change something in order that your brain can respond.

And in the same way, if you are physically energised, your brain will then fire better.

To my complete delight, I saw a fantastic manifestation of the theory when chairing the Pendulum Summit in the National Convention Centre in Dublin.

By mid afternoon the energy had left the room. The 2,000 delegates, listening since 8.30am were flagging, so I needed to do something to energise them before the headline act, Deepak Chopra. But we were running well over time, so it would have to be something quick! I whispered to Norma Murphy, the floor manager, to trust me and I started into a little exercise.

I asked everyone to stand up, and then to slump over, hanging their shoulders and their heads down, and to say in the lowest, saddest voice they could muster, "I am very happy."

It was actually great fun to see the whole convention obliging, going along with me, without knowing where this was going.

And then I asked them to throw their arms in the air, to stretch up as far as they could go, and to shout at the tops of their voices "I am very sad".

Well if you are so sad, I asked them, why are you all laughing?

And indeed, people were laughing, probably at the silliness of the exercise, but also appreciative of the change in the whole atmosphere in the room.

We each have to find the things that work for us – the energiser, the mood changer, the uplifter – the action that allows us to disconnect the cogs, and to go off in a different direction or at a different speed when we re-connect the cogs. And if for you that doesn't happen to be fresh air and exercise it can be:

- Taking a class in something new, like Japanese or economics
- Creating a vision board, or painting a picture
- Helping out a local charity
- Doing something for a friend in need
- Writing in your journal
- Watching an inspiring TED talk
- Reading a great book
- Making a bucket list
- Making a gratitude list

The point is that oscillation between activities allows us to be more productive.

'All work and no play makes Jack a dull boy,' so the old saying goes, and undoubtedly repeating the same activities over and over will drain us and leave us with that feeling of running on empty. The more we try to fit into an already over crowded day, the less we are likely to actually get done.

Francesco Cirillo's Pomodoro Technique is a great one to try if you ever suffer from a feeling of disgruntlement at the end of a long and difficult day, that you didn't quite achieve enough, despite your best efforts.

The technique uses a red tomato shaped timer – physical or online, whichever you prefer – to allow you to really focus in a concentrated way for a short burst of time, and then to give your self that oscillation in the form of a short break, mental and physical.

So you set the timer for 25 minutes, and concentrate furiously on the task at hand – the report you are trying to write, the project that has to be completed, and when the timer goes off you stop completely, note what you have achieved and take a three to five minute break. The break should involve walking away from the task, and doing a few stretches or something else to pump the blood.

After four pomodori, or 25 minute work segments, you take a longer break of 15 to 30 minutes. Devotees of the technique swear by it, and have noticed huge increases in their productivity.

Author and speaker Dr Heidi Hanna has taken the concept of oscillation to another level with her research on brain training for optimal performance and output. In her books *The Sharp Solution* and *Stressoholic* she details how too much stress and not enough recovery time – along with poor diet, not enough exercise, and not enough real connection with those around us – actually causes the destruction of the brain.

And she spells out programmes you can put in place to get your brain into a better place to withstand the pressures of modern day living through recovery, rebalancing and recharging.

"Everything about the human system is designed to oscillate – from heartbeats to brainwaves and blood sugar," she explains. "Yet most people flat-line their way throughout the day, overriding our natural patterns in an attempt to get more done in less time.

"As a result, we depend on stress hormones and stimulation to keep our systems energised which ultimately causes us to break down and burnout. The simple solution is to manage energy more effectively by living life as a series of sprints rather than a marathon. Studies have shown that breaks as short as 3-5 minutes can help to balance brain chemistry, build brain health and boost brainpower!"

I have found Heidi's work in this area absolutely fascinating, and the best argument for minding the diet and taking more exercise I have ever come across – the positive gains in performance and output a much better carrot than any notions of air-brushed perfection.

But of course the knowing/doing gap features in here again. We all know what we should be doing, but actually getting around to doing it is another thing entirely, unless you are very disciplined.

"Like many CEOs I used to be a workaholic, confronting all of life's problems with the belief that I could fix them with more hours at the office", says Rory Geoghegan, of Red Box Direct. "But fostering a culture of long hours wasn't good for my business, staff, family or for myself – so I changed.

"I discovered exercise and how it could make me more productive. Now I hit the gym in the middle of every day and return to the office invigorated. Post-lunch used to be a grind. Now I get the buzzing energy of the morning twice every day.

"The realisation that being present and being productive are not the same thing has been an eye-opener and as a result I have become uncompromising in my commitment to my exercise programme. Now I have time for work, my family and for me. It all gets done!"

On a panel recently on Newstalk radio we were asked to comment on a new report from the World Health Organisation, which claimed that Ireland will be the most obese country in Europe by the year 2030. As many as 85 per cent of women are set to be overweight by that time and a shocking 57 per cent obese. Irish men weren't any better with 89 per cent predicted to be overweight and 48 per cent obese.

I said that the report had popped the movie *Wall.E* straight into my head, a cataclysmic distopian scenario where the whole overweight nation would have to go around on motorised chairs.

It is hard to know how accurate these projections are, but one thing is for sure: The worldwide property and banking crash of September 2007 impacted more in Ireland than anywhere else, both in terms of actual monetary loss – proportionate to GDP – and in the effect on mental health and well-being. The incidence of death by suicide among the business community was unprecedented.

The people who ticked the boxes in the WHO survey, and on whom the projections were based, are a people emerging out of a national depression that put survival far ahead of immediate health.

One entrepreneur I know freely admits that he has consoled himself unstintingly over the past few years with food and drink. He says that it is only now – with his banking issues nearing some kind of a resolution – that he is thinking about his health and fitness again, emerging blinking into the sunlight like a bear coming out of his cave.

Psychologists will say that some people naturally have more resilience than others, but will equally argue that we can all develop more of it. It all depends on how much we accept that adversity is a normal part of life, and how much we are prepared or able to adjust to new circumstances, and look for the good in them.

So if we are to be healthily resilient, we have to accept the bad but balance it with the good, training the little voice in the head to say that this part of my life may be in shreds, but I still have this and this and this to be thankful about.

In *Flourishing*, Maureen Gaffney describes the 5:1 ratio of good experiences to bad we need to really thrive in life. Every little niggle or worry or put-down or call from a bank is a negative that needs to be countered with three indications of affection, or pleasant thoughts about an upcoming event or holiday, or signs of appreciation from someone. And that's just to keep us on an even keel!

To really flourish we need to find five positives to balance each negative. And we can't rely on others for the positives. We have to find ways of giving ourselves the positives, without resorting to chocolate or wine!

This can be done by reminding ourselves every day of the things we should be grateful for. Yes, it is a bit of a Facebook fad at the moment to post 'gratitude' notes but there is science behind it, so it is not as corny as it looks. Consciously noting and appreciating the good things as we go along makes us emotionally stronger, and better able to withstand the bad things.

A constantly cheerful business development coach I know has a 'gratitude' file on the left of her screen, in there with all the projects she is currently working on. Every time she gets stressed, or feels it is all coming at her like a train, she opens the file, reads some of the things she has put there before, and adds in a new one.

She swears it immediately drops her blood pressure, focuses her, and allows her return to her tasks ready to go again. And the best thing is that kind of break has no calories!

Resilience is also fostered by a willingness to learn and an openness to new things. None of us is ever fully 'cooked'. We are works in progress, and the day you decide you know it all is the day you start to make the road really long and hard for yourself.

Instead, if you start looking for learning in everything, even the bad stuff, you are training your brain for adaptability and agility, and ultimately happiness and success.

So you might ask yourself what have I learned from this situation? What do I now know about myself that I didn't before? How can I use this experience into the future? How can I make sure that others don't have to face what I did?

Learning to deal with stuff is what makes us who we are. Every challenge we have successfully overcome has grown our confidence, strengthened our will, given us the notion that we can tackle things head on in the future – qualities we would never have developed if we had not had the difficulties in the first place.

I sometimes think that the only thing we really, really need to give our children is the ability to solve problems, because if they can do that, everything else will fall into place. If we can get them to believe that they probably will be able to work out what to do, in most sets of circumstances, they will be unstoppable.

And that's not to say they should have an unrealistic belief in their abilities, but more that they should trust themselves to cope with whatever might come along, and not to be pole-axed with shock that bad things are out there in the first place.

Another big part of developing and fostering resilience is a healthy and active community; the people who are there for you, who have your back, and who share and understand your experiences. There are friends you have a laugh with, friends you have a moan with, friends you drink too much wine with, and friends who support you, and we need them all.

At the start of this book I mentioned Family Forum. I based

the development of the system on the monthly Forum I attend as part of my membership of the worldwide Entrepreneur's Organisation. My Forum gives me the support kind of friendship from a group of like-minded business people who I know, at this stage of the game, would walk over coals for me.

Every month, we closet ourselves in a room for a few hours, and go through a set of protocols where we share our issues in our business and personal lives, confident that no one will judge, or give advice, or talk about anything they hear outside the room.

Entrepreneurs hate to be told what to do. So you learn from experience that is shared. Your colleagues might have had a similar situation in the past, so they tell you about it, rather than telling you what to do. You can take or leave the information, but ultimately you decide yourself how you are going to solve the problem.

I think the value of an opportunity like the one I have just described is in the real and meaningful bonds that develop. They are the perfect antidote to thousands of 'likes' from people who may well be very interested in you, and supportive in their own way, but who are not a very central part of your life.

Social media is a lot of fun, and a great way to create some 'white noise' around your product or service, but it also alienates people and creates a lot of loneliness – every one else appearing to have a happier, glossier, more successful life than your own.

But life is not a see-saw. You are not down because someone else is up. So there is no need to let pictures of weddings and exotic travel and successful people incite Facebook envy. Or no need to let social media weaken your resilience muscle.

Use it instead to find and share stories of people who have overcome great odds, and who inspire us every day with their own positivity, adaptability and refusal to let adversity hold them back.

Jack Kavanagh, the young TEDx speaker I referred to earlier, was setting off to go sky-diving in the USA, and to make a documentary about it, when I asked him for a comment for this section of the book.

"If I'm honest the last number of years I have been getting through on instinct, just surviving a bit better every day. After such a big trauma in my life I felt that my passions, and everything I knew, had been taken from me because it was hard for me to interact with them in the same way under my new circumstances.

"Since my injury I have been constantly striving to lead the most normal life I can, and so when I saw my friends go travelling it was an obvious thing for me to want to do. I'm lucky that I have an optimistic outlook and that I see possibilities rather than problems.

"The desire to lead as normal a life as I can, not to sit and wallow because I was thrown a challenge, and the will to rediscover passion is what has driven me forward in the last few years. As for the skydive – maybe my normal is a bit different to yours!"

Jack is inspirational in his determination to keep on doing all the things 23-year-old students are supposed to do. His goals and ambitions are completely intact, and he is clearly going to keep ticking that bucket list, one item at a time.

The great American baseball coach Tommy Lasorda said: "The difference between the possible and the impossible lies in a person's determination," and Jack certainly has the determination.

I recently heard ambitions and goals described as shiny pennies, and I thought it was very apt. You have to scatter them there on the table in front of you, and play around with them until you can see some order, until they start to stack up, and things fall into place for you.

So you do a brain dump of all the things you want to do – like writing the book, or recording the song, or running the marathon, or changing the job – putting down everything that comes into your head with absolutely no self-limits or self-doubt allowed.

These are the shiny pennies, and the list could be quite long and quite out there!

But by simply writing the list, you are admitting to yourself that you do actually want these things, and there is a part of your brain telling you loudly that you are quite capable of achieving them.

So now you have to decide in what order are you going to tackle the things on the list. Or in other words, which of the pennies is the shiniest, the most appealing, the closest to your heart? Which of the things do you really want to go after now? And where is the ladder that is going to lead to that goal?

Doing some communications training recently with a group of aspiring politicians, I asked them to discuss ambition. It took quite a bit of pushing, but eventually a few of them admitted that they would quite like to be Taoiseach one day.

So I drew a ladder on the flip chart, put the words Taoiseach on the top, and we started working out the rungs of the ladder going down – party leader, government minister, junior minister, TD, party convention nominee, party member, local councillor, student politics and so on.

Some of the group was not even on the first rung of the ladder then, but the exercise was useful for them, and they could see clearly what they had to do. Don't get put off by how far away the top of the mountain is, concentrate on getting up to the next ledge.

And you are far more likely to get the help and support you need to climb to the next ledge, if you are looking, acting and sounding like a leader, long before you actually reach that pay grade.

Body language, personal mannerisms and the way we use language can sometimes give away personal power. Aspiring leaders need to avoid the signals that display unease or lack of confidence to others.

The physical signals that reduce the perception of personal power include poor posture, lack of eye contact, shifting weight from foot to foot, looking stressed or harried, touching the face or playing with the hair.

The verbal signals include things like deflecting compliments, self-deprecation, confiding insecurities, speaking too fast or too slow, taking too long to get to the point and using hesitant or weak language.

The opposite is of course to practise giving out strong verbal and physical signals which protect your personal power.

This includes taking credit where it is due, knowing what you want and asking for it, using decisive language, speaking up, having clear views, understanding the difference between assertiveness and aggression, knowing when to say no, and understanding the sources and uses of power within the group or organisation.

Remember Paul Boross's advice above about getting your physiology right? Some people call this 'faking it till you make it' or in other words, acting the way you want to be perceived. Because if you act like you are confident, and in control, you will firstly be perceived in that way, and then you will actually become that way.

And taking that logic forward, if you act like a leader you will be perceived as one, and you will eventually become one.

But no matter how big your ambitions are, don't ever let them distract you from giving your all at your current level. You get promoted because of how well you are doing your current role, not because you are letting everyone know you are not focusing on it, because you really believe you are too good for it.

Acting like a leader means delivering results daily, so that nobody around you – above, below or to the side – has reason to ever question your performance. It means offering to carry an extra load, taking on additional projects that are in themselves fulfilling but which also signal your leadership potential.

It's about finding role models and mentors within the group, and working to support their projects and goals so you can learn from them.

It's about finding and recognising your blind spots, so you get some training and development in those areas, or at very least you can find work-arounds, until the time comes when you can employ someone to do that aspect of the work.

It's about networking and building strong relationships so that people already know what you are like and what you are capable of, long before you sit across from them at the interview board.

♦   ♦   ♦

The path to becoming a performing leader is wide open to anyone who chooses to take it. Achieving that elusive executive presence we spoke about at the start of the book, or the kind of gravitas that makes people listen to and really connect with what you are saying, is completely achievable. By you. Now.

But it takes dedication, plenty of practice and a little luck. And remember, the harder you work, the luckier you get.

The funny thing is that those who get there usually never really accept that they have done so. They are committed to life-long learning and continuous self-development, so they are always looking to nudge their personal bar just that little bit higher.

Thank you for reading *Perform As a Leader*, and I hope to meet you in person some day to hear about your own road to success.

Index

About the Author

ORLAITH CARMODY is the Managing Director of Mediatraining.ie, which specialises in communications training and leadership development. In demand as a keynote speaker, conference chair and seminar leader, she has addressed Ireland's most influential business people, networks and political groups. She has also presented at conferences in the USA, UAE, Canada and all over Europe.

An active media commentator, she contributes regularly to a variety of programmes and publications on subjects such as doing business today, women's participation at board level and in public life, entrepreneurship, education and parenting.

Following a career as a broadcast journalist with RTÉ, Orlaith became a serial entrepreneur, and is a director of a number of SMEs in media, recruitment, production and education. She served on the board of RTÉ from 2010 to 2015.

She is a founder member of the Irish Chapter of EO, the Entrepreneurs' Organisation, and was President 2014/15.

She lives on the Louth–Meath border with her husband and business partner, Gavin Duffy, and their four children, now young adults.

The Perform Programme

NOW that you have finished the book, why not log on to Orlaith's web page to learn more about how you can *Perform As A Leader* by joining the Perform Programme community.

www.PerformAsALeader.com

IT is a great way to reinforce the learning, to access new material and to have your individual questions answered.

You can take the Perform Programme online, if you wish, or just join the community to hear how others are doing, and to tell us how you are getting on yourself. Take a minute to upload your question or idea, and Orlaith will address it as soon as she can.

Members of the Perform community will also receive additional free material every so often, to compliment the contents of the book and the programme, and to keep you up to date on the latest techniques and tools in leadership performance.

We love feedback, and will be really looking forward to hearing from you!

Follow us on Twitter @performleader

And on Facebook: www.facebook.com/performasaleader